CHINESE COOKING

THE EASY WOK METHOD

Karen Lee Aland

Illustrations by Bob Kelly

Cover design by Irene Rubin

Cover photograph by Fred N. Grayson

Editorial Assistant: Anne Saidman

ISBN 0-913880-06-X
Copyright © 1977 by
Trafalgar House Publishing, Inc.

Trafalgar House Publishing, Inc.
460 East 79th Street
New York, N.Y. 10021

CONTENTS

CHINESE COOKING

1. INTRODUCTION TO CHINESE COOKING

Why another Chinese cookbook?

When I first decided to write this book, I decided to attempt to solve a major problem that Western chefs face when preparing Chinese meals.

If you have ever attempted Chinese cooking, or if you have observed the food being prepared, you will quickly realize that there is as much art in the preparation of the food as there is in the cooking. But these are skills, and skills can easily be taught.

What is more difficult to learn, and something rarely, if ever, discussed in the many cookbooks available, is the technique of combining food, how to prepare an entire meal, or what dishes go with what other dishes. If you are serving Shrimp with Snow Peas, what other dishes should accompany it? Will the meal be too bland if you are serving it with Chicken Velvet? Will the mild flavor emerge if you are serving Spicy Pork with Vermicelli, or should you serve Beef with Oyster Sauce?

The Chinese chef never asks these questions — it's a matter of instinct. But the Westerner has not been brought up with these instincts and rarely has she been exposed to Chinese cooking all her life. Thus, we have all made errors of selection in Chinese restaurants, and have made the same mistakes in preparing Chinese meals for our friends.

This book groups foods together into typical menus. As you progress through the book you will become more familiar with the tastes and combinations of foods that are acceptable to the pallate.

Hopefully, there will come a time when you can look in your pantry and refrigerator, and whip together a meal for two or a sumptuous banquet for twelve. You will also know how many dishes to prepare, what to buy, and, most important to the success of the meal — what goes with what!

2. CHARACTERISTICS OF CHINESE FOOD/COOKING

The problem of "what goes with what" is undoubtedly created by the variety of foods and the many regional tastes available to us.

There are six basic flavors in Chinese cooking — pungent, salty, sweet, sour, spicy, and bitter. These flavors come from the many provinces and regions of China. Essentially, there are four major regions, with each one having its own cooking style: Peking (north), Cantonese (south), Shanghai (east), and Szechwan (west or southwest). Many of the other types of foods that have become popular, such as Hunan, are included in these areas.

For years, the only type of Chinese cooking Americans were familiar with was Cantonese, since the Cantonese were the first to migrate to the west. Eventually all the other areas came to be represented.

We know these different *schools* of cooking by the variety of tastes and spices used in preparation. Styles of cooking are dictated by the availability of foods in that area. The seacoast area of Canton provides plentiful fish, and its climate is ideal for agriculture. In the Szechuan region, the climate is far better suited for growing spices and mushrooms, and today we often equate Szechuan cooking with hot, spicy food.

Thus, it is the harmonious and delicate blending of these tastes and textures that makes Chinese food as interesting as it has become. The Chinese in small villages often have a limited variety of ingredients with which to work and do not have a wide assortment of dishes available to them. We are more fortunate. This book contemplates a variety of tastes and styles that will please the pallate and help to develop an appreciation for the broad range of recipes that have made their way to this country. This proper balancing of these recipes will make you a "master" Chinese chef.

11

3. TOOLS OF THE CHEF

Although you can use many of the utensils found in the kitchen for Chinese cooking, your work will be easier and far more efficient if you acquire some of the basic tools of the Chinese chef.

THE WOK

The wok is considered essential to most Chinese cooking. Although you may often substitute an ordinary skillet for your food preparation, the flexibility of the wok is unmatched by any other utensil.

The round bottom of the wok offers several cooking advantages. The cooking oil collects at the bottom of the wok, permitting high temperature, efficient cooking without soaking in the oil. The high, smooth, sloping sides are excellent for stir frying, and to prevent food from spilling as might be the case with an ordinary frying pan. A thin, yet heavy, iron wok is preferred and can be purchased in a Chinese market or in many department stores throughout the country.

There are two styles of wok — one with a long handle, and one with iron handles on both sides. Use whichever type is easier for you to manage.

When buying a wok, consider the size of your stove. If the wok is too large, pots won't fit on the other burners next to the wok.

A wok ring often accompanies the wok. This is a circular metal ring to be placed over a burner. The rounded bottom of the wok fits into this ring and prevents the wok from sliding around or tilting on the stove. However, since the ring raises the wok above the burner, it is necessary to rest the wok directly on the stove when a higher heat source is necessary.

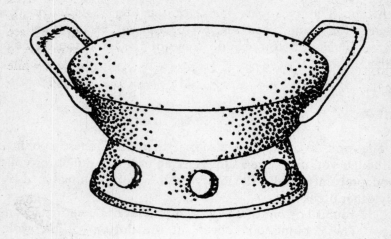

The wok cover is a useful accompaniment to your wok. Not only will it help keep food warm, but it is essential when steaming food in the wok.

Seasoning the wok is necessary and easy to do. Heat one half cup of cooking oil in your freshly scrubbed wok, over a low heat. Let it heat for a half hour, occasionally tilting the wok so the oil flows around the entire surface. Pour off the oil, wash and dry the wok, and you are finished. It is now ready for use.

To clean the wok, you may use a Chinese wok cleaner, which is made from a sheaf of bamboo slivers bound together at one end. Run water into the hot wok, and loosen any food or oil that sticks to the bottom or sides using the wok cleaner or a nylon scrub pad. If you are going to use the wok again to prepare another dish, wipe it dry with a rag and place it back on the fire. If you are through, merely clean it and wipe it dry. Rust is the only thing that will ruin your wok, so never store it while it is still wet.

LADLE AND SPATULA

There are two cooking utensils that are traditionally used with the wok: the long-handled spoon or ladle, and the spatula, which is a flat metal spoon with curved sides. Both tools are used to stir foods, and in addition Chinese chefs use the ladle to transfer oil, soy sauce, and other ingredients to the wok while cooking. A wooden spatula or flat spoon can also be used.

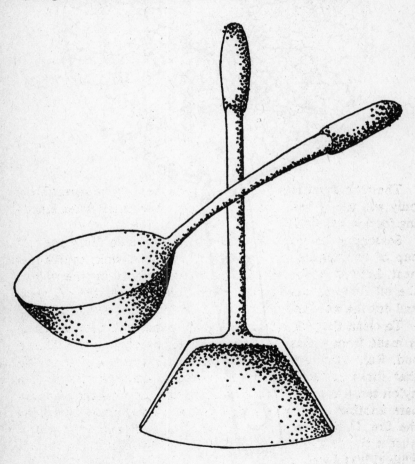

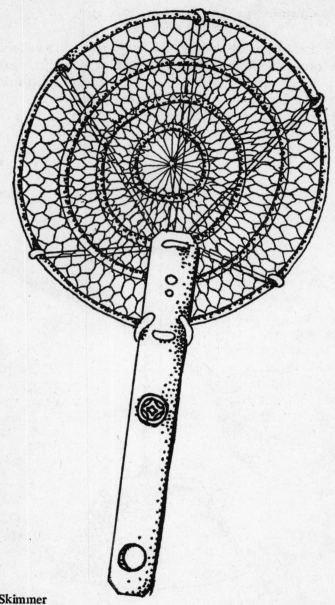

Wire Skimmer

WIRE SKIMMER

The wire skimmer is usually made of twisted wire attached to a long wooden handle. It comes in various sizes and is useful in removing foods cooked in deep oil. Hold the skimmer over the wok to let the oil drip through the wire frame.

OIL DRAINER

This piece of equipment is optional but handy. When frying foods, the entire contents of the wok may be dumped into the oil drainer. After the oil has run off, the food can be returned to the wok or dish.

STEAMERS

Steaming is a very important part of Chinese cooking, and bamboo steamers are excellent for this. They come in layers which permit several different types of foods to be prepared at the same time. Chinese appetizers, such as dim sum (steamed dumplings), can be prepared and served in the same bamboo steamer. Flat, metal steamer dishes are also available for use with the wok and can be used for steaming large items, such as duck.

COOKING CHOPSTICKS

Although these are not essential, they are often useful for retrieving pieces of ginger or garlic from the bubbling wok, for stirring a corn starch mixture, and for turning certain foods.

17

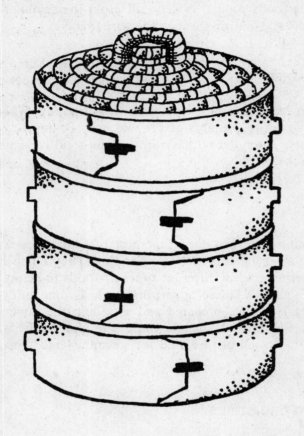

Bamboo Steamer Trays

18

CLEAVER

No discussion of cooking equipment would be complete without the Chinese chef's right hand — the cleaver. Although a regular sharp kitchen knife may be used, cutting, chopping, dicing, slicing, and mincing are made much easier with the cleaver.

Cleavers come in three sizes — heavy, medium, and light weight. The medium weight will probably suit most purposes. Carbon steel will hold its edge far longer than stainless steel, and can be easily sharpened. When you buy the cleaver, make sure it feels comfortable in your hand, since you will be using it to prepare almost everything.

Sharpen the cleaver occasionally on a whetstone or a kitchen sharpening rod.

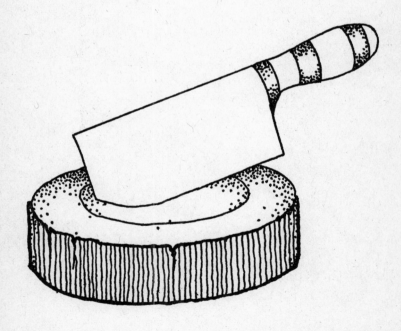

CHOPPING BLOCK

While most Chinese cooks use a thick wooden slab from a hardwood tree trunk, any good cutting board will do. Since you are using a cleaver and often will be chopping through an entire chicken or duck, the block should be heavy enough not to slip off the table. Also, the surface should be wide enough to hold a large quantity of food. Clean the board with a nylon scrub brush and soap and water.

4. INGREDIENT PREPARATION

There is no step in cooking Chinese food that is more important than ingredient preparation. This is your key to success. Aside from the fact that uniformity looks better when a dish is served, it assures proper doneness of the food.

The three essentials to keep in mind are: the size of the ingredients, the thickness, and the required cooking time unique to the individual ingredients that are called for. A carrot strip will require longer to cook than a snow pea. If the carrot is cut into matchstick-sized shreds, the cooking time is vastly reduced, and the carrots and peas will be cooked to the proper doneness. The major vegetables and meats are cut to similar size and shape in most stir-fried Chinese recipes, to unify the required cooking time.

There are six basic cutting methods for food preparation — slicing, shredding, dicing or cubing, scoring, roll cutting, and chopping.

Slicing is used for both meats and vegetables. All the major ingredients in a dish should be of uniform size and thickness. Slicing meat is easier if the meat is partially frozen. This prevents the meat from slipping under the knife. Meat should be cut across the grain in 1/8 inch slices.

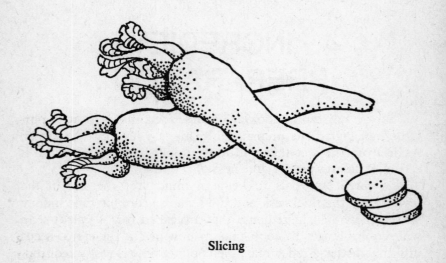

Slicing

Vegetables may be cut across, or at an angle to expose more inner surface and increase the tenderness. This is where the roll cut would be used. Cutting vegetables in this manner will make stir-frying easier, since the pieces won't stick together in the wok.

Shredding is, in effect, double slicing. The thin slices are stacked and then sliced once more. Foods cut in this manner will cook quickly. Shredding is usually described in three sizes: matchstick, double matchstick, and triple matchstick size, depending on how narrowly the food is sliced the second time.

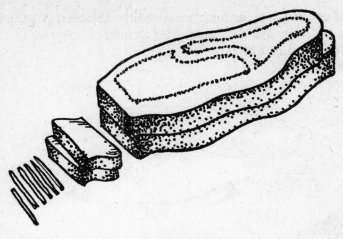

Shredding

When food is to be cubed or diced, you first start by cutting large cubes. Dicing requires smaller pieces than cubing, no larger than 3/8 of an inch square, so cut the cubes into smaller pieces. The recipe will designate the size which depends on the nature of the food being cooked and the cooking time desired.

Scoring is a method of cutting which is used on larger pieces of meat. Shallow cuts are evenly spaced on the top of the meat at intervals, first in one direction and then at an angle to those cuts, thus forming diamond patterns.

This allows the seasoning to get into the meat, which cooks more quickly and becomes more tender. It also adds to the meat's appearance.

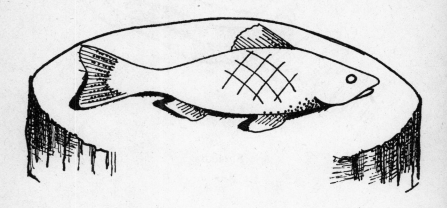

Scoring

Chopping and mincing are used constantly in Chinese cooking. Both involve cutting the food into the smallest possible bits for ease in mixing and speed in cooking.

Roll cutting is a method of cutting tough, fiberous vegetables such as carrots and asparagus. The vegetable is sliced at an angle, then it is rolled 1/4 of an inch and sliced at an angle in the opposite direction.

Roll Cutting

5. METHODS OF COOKING

Chinese cooking techniques vary with the type and nature of the food that is being cooked, how it is cut, and the flavor effect that is desired.

STIR-FRYING

This the the Chinese equivilant of sautéing. It demands a high temperature, and the ingredients must constantly be stirred with a small amount of oil. Stir-frying requires constant attention, and for this reason all the ingredients and seasonings should be at hand before the cooking commences, when this method is used.

Foods cooked in this manner are usually cut into uniform sizes and thicknesses. They require only a few minutes of cooking and should be served immediately. Stir-frying enhances the color and taste of vegetables, preserving their texture.

SHALLOW FRYING

This method is different from stir-frying in that more oil and a medium high heat are used, and the food is only turned once or twice during the frying period. Shallow frying is used quite often to brown meat in order to seal in the juices.

DEEP FRYING

The food being cooked is totally immersed in very hot oil — generally 350 to 375 degrees. To avoid spattering, foods should be relatively dry when put into the oil. In some cases, such as when meat is wet from marinade or light batter, the heat can be lowered slightly before introducing the food. If the heat is too low, however, the food will become oily and soggy. It is important that the food being cooked in this manner be relatively thin. If the nature of the food makes this impossible, it should be pre-cooked. For example, a chicken leg may become too crisp on the outside and completely uncooked next to the bone if it is deep fried without being pre-cooked.

RED STEWING

This is a long and slow cooking process. The food is placed in water or broth with soy sauce and seasonings. Red stewing is uniquely Chinese and it is especially useful in cooking tough cuts of meat. The cooking time varies with the type of meat, but it is usually over one hour and can be up to 5 or 6 hours for shin of beef.

The flavor is subtle and this method can be used for cold as well as hot dishes.

STEAMING

The food is placed on a bamboo rack or a metal steaming dish with holes in the bottom. A small amount of water is poured into the bottom of the wok. The rack rests above the water, which is brought to a boil. The wok is then covered to seal in the steam, and then the heat is lowered slightly. Steaming requires little attention, and, if your equipment is so designed, several tiers can be placed over the water to be steamed simultaneously.

Cooking in this way, at a lower temperature, preserves food nutrients and flavor. It is also useful in reheating meats and leftovers. Food should be brought to room temperature before steaming, otherwise condensation will occur, making your food too soggy.

POACHING

This method is especially useful for preparing fish. The liquid, which can be either broth or water, is seasoned and heated to just below the boiling point. The meat is immersed and simmered until done.

BOILING

Enough water, and a pot large enough for the food to float freely are required. Parboiling is used frequently for longer-cooking vegetables used in stir-fried combinations. The water is brought to a boil and vegetables are added. When the water returns to a boil, remove the vegetables.

BARBECUING

An outdoor cooking method that uses charcoal heat, this can be used year-round in warm climates, and during the summer in most other places. The food is placed on a rotisserie, spit, or grill above the charcoal. The coal imparts an excellent flavor to meats.

ROASTING

Simply cook the meat in an oven with frequent basting. For fatty meats, such as pork and duck, the meat can be hung over a pan with a little water in it. The water keeps the meat moist. Cut up wire hangers to make the hooks, bend the pieces into an "S" shape with a pair of pliers, and push the hooks through the meat. Just watch your fingers as the hooks come out the other side.

COLD-MIX

This method does not require heat. It is the preparation of a dish by mixing prepared, cold ingredients. The textures of the foods being mixed change somewhat after the mixing. For example, if a cooked meat is mixed with shredded lettuce and sesame oil, this will soften the crispness and reduce the volume of lettuce.

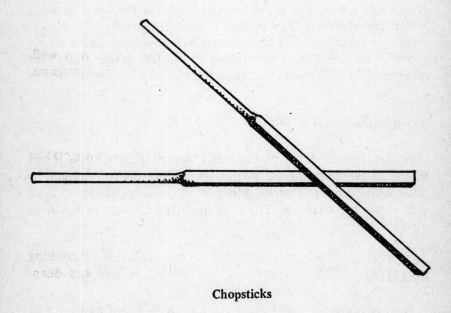

Chopsticks

6. THE CHINESE MENU

The Chinese menu is a planned artistic presentation. A balance of color and texture with an harmonious variety of tastes and types of foods are the essentials for the menu you serve.

Your menu usually includes the two standards of any Chinese meal; rice and soup, along with main dishes selected according to the following considerations:

VARIETY OF TEXTURES

Shredded, crisp and crunchy vegetables with smooth sauces, tender chewy meats, soft bean curd, or crispy fried meats.

VARIETY OF TASTES

Sweet and sour, pungent, salty, spicy, and bitter. Any well-planned menu will include several of these taste characteristics.

VARIETY OF INGREDIENTS

Meats, poultry seafood, rice, noodles, and various vegetables of different colors, textures and tastes.

VARIETY OF COOKING METHODS

For ease of preparation, a menu should include slow cooking recipes and cold-mixed as well as stir-fried recipes and deep-fried recipes.

This is difficult to judge. The Chinese meal is always served "family-style." The best guage is to prepare one dish per person, plus rice. For a group of four: soup, three meat and/or vegetable dishes, and rice.

If there are six guests, you should plan to have a soup, five other dishes, and rice. Instead of five different dishes you may want to increase quantities and make fewer recipes. If quantities are increased in a recipe remember to stir-fry half the required amount of the vegetables in the wok at a time; otherwise, they will cook too slowly and become soggy and overcooked. If too much meat is stir-fried, it will become watery. You will find that a larger wok will be helpful in avoiding these problems.

Cold-mix dishes can easily be doubled and recipes using slow-cook procedures can easily be increased.

Once you have selected the dishes for your menu, you may then focus your attention on organizing its preparation.

Make a list of the ingredients and quantities needed for all the recipes. Be certain that you have everything required to prepare the meal. Determine which recipes can be made in advance, which sauces can be pre-mixed and which ingredients can be chopped or sliced a day in advance. Canned ingredients such as bamboo shoots and water chestnuts can be prepared the day before. You can store mushrooms in water in the refrigerator. The meats which are to be marinated can be cut and placed in the marinade ahead of time. Broth for soup can be made a day or two in advance if you prefer this to the canned varieties, although all Chinese chefs keep a supply of soup stock on hand at all times. Fresh vegetables, however, must be *very fresh* and should not be chopped or cut the day before cooking.

If you are feeding other people, rather than just yourself, plan the order in which you will cook the dishes, the serving platters you will need, and how you will set the table. If you feel that you will be too rushed bringing everything to the table at once, break the meal into segments. For example, when serving Moo Shu Pork with pancakes, steam the pancakes and stir-fry the Moo Shu Pork, and make this the first course. While this is being enjoyed, a cold mixed dish is served. The rice is cooking, the red-stewed chicken is being re-heated, the soup is simmering, and the meat and vegetable dishes can be stir-fried to serve with the remainder of the meal. You can easily feed 6 to 8 people with a minimum of chaos.

Your menu is now complete, and planned as an experience to please both sight and taste.

MENUS AND RECIPES

7. FIRST RECIPES FOR THE NOVICE

Now you are ready to begin cooking, and start on your way to becoming an expert Chinese chef.

These first recipes for the novice will give you practical — and rewarding — experience utilizing basic methods. It's your chance to familiarize yourself with the utensils, ingredients, and seasonings frequently used in the preparation of Chinese dishes. The techniques will be explained in detail.

Basic Recipes in this Chapter

The Sesame Fish
Chinese Meatballs
Basic Chicken Broth
Egg Flower Soup
Bean Curd Soup
Perfect Boiled Rice
Almond Fried Rice
Beef Congee
Shrimp with Onions in
    Black Bean Sauce
Shrimp with Snow Peas
Steamed Fish
Stir-Fried Chicken with
    Bean Sprouts

Red-Stewed Chicken
Beef with Onions
Stir-Fried Beef with Peppers
Hoisin Pork
Pork with Cashew Nuts
Stir-Fried Spinach with Bacon
Broccoli Stems with
    Soy Sauce
Braised Chinese Cabbage
Stir-fried String Beans
Sweet and Sour Carrots
Beef Lo Mein
Szechwanese Pork Vermicelli
Almond Tea

THE SESAME FISH

This tasty appetizer will be a favorite for both Chinese and Western menus. A fillet of sole or flounder may be used. If you cannot buy the shallots, scallions may be substituted. Ginger and sherry subdue the fishy odor and add a subtle flavor. The coating made with cornstarch will be crispy.

First put the wok ring on the burner and place the wok securely on it for deep frying. Deep frying in this way will require 3 cups of vegetable, corn, or peanut oil.

INGREDIENTS:
1 pound fish fillets with all
   the skin removed and cut
   into 2-inch squares
   $\frac{3}{8}$ inches thick
2 Tablespoons cornstarch
1 egg lightly beaten
Sesame seeds, unroasted
Oil for deep-frying

MARINADE:
3 slices ginger, minced
2 shallots, minced
2 Tablespoons sherry
1 teaspoon sugar
dash of salt and pepper

WOKCOOK:
   1. Marinate the fish pieces in the minced ginger, shallots, sherry, sugar, salt, and pepper for 15 to 30 minutes.
   2. Lightly coat each piece of fish with cornstarch, then dip it in the egg and roll it in the sesame seeds.
   3. Heat the oil to a moderately hot temperature of 250° to 300°. Deep fry the pieces of fish until they are a golden color and remove them from the wok with your strainer.

Serve with a mixture of 3 Tablespoons commercial duck sauce, 1 teaspoon Chinese mustard, and 1 teaspoon soy sauce.
   Serves 6.

CHINESE MEATBALLS

These little meatballs can be prepared in advance and reheated to serve. To reheat them, deep-fry briefly and place in a hot oven for a few minutes with a little soy sauce sprinkled over them.

INGREDIENTS:
1½ pound pork ground
4 black mushrooms soaked in boiling water for 20 minutes. Remove the stems and chop them finely
½ cup bamboo shoots, finely minced
½ cup bean sprouts, finely minced
1 leaf of Chinese cabbage, finely minced
1 cup scallions, minced
(press the excess water out of the above vegetables)
1 egg
2 Tablespoons cornstarch
1 egg beaten
Oil for deep frying

SEASONINGS:
1 garlic clove, crushed
1 Tablespoon fresh ginger, minced
a pinch of cayenne (red pepper)

WOKCOOK:
1. Mix all ingredients and seasonings except the beaten egg and cornstarch. Form into balls the size of a walnut.
2. Roll them in the egg and then briefly in the cornstarch.
3. Deep fry them until they are well done.

Serve with a sauce made of soy sauce and mustard.
Serves 6 to 8.

CHICKEN BROTH

This recipe for chicken broth can be used in all recipes using broth as an ingredient.

INGREDIENTS:
3 pound chicken, cleaned
  and quartered
1 scallion

SEASONINGS:
1 slice ginger, minced
½ teaspoon salt

COOK:
1. Cover a quartered chicken with water and bring it to a boil.
2. Remove the chicken and discard this water and rinse the chicken.
3. Bring 3 quarts of water to a boil and add the chicken. Simmer the chicken, scallions, and ginger for 4 hours. Add ½ teaspoon salt, then remove and discard the chicken.
4. Cool the broth. Freeze immediately for future use or refrigerate for use within 3 days.

Serves 6

EGG FLOWER SOUP

This velvet-smooth soup is commonly called "egg drop soup." If you like this basic soup, try the deluxe version, Hot and Sour Soup.

INGREDIENTS:
3 eggs, lightly beaten with
  3 teaspoons water
3 scallions (green tops
  only) chopped
5 teaspoons cornstarch dissolved in 4 Tablespoons
  water
8 cups chicken broth

SEASONINGS:
1 teaspoon sugar
1 teaspoon salt
2 teaspoons sherry
1½ Tablespoons soy sauce

WOKCOOK:

1. Dissolve the cornstarch in ⅓ cup of the cold broth.

2. Bring the rest of the broth to a boil, then add the corn-starch mixture and return the soup to a boil.

3. Reduce the heat and add sugar, salt, sherry and the soy sauce.

4. Pour in the eggs in a slow stream. Stir slowly and they will separate into shreds.

Serve garnished with the scallions or slivered ham.
Serves 6.

BEAN CURD SOUP

Bean curd cakes and bean sprouts are low calorie, high protein foods. An excellent meal if you are watching your calories.

INGREDIENTS:
6 cups chicken broth
6 black mushrooms soaked in
boiling water for 15 to 30
minutes, remove the stems
and slice thinly
2 fresh bean curd cakes cut
into ½ inch cubes
1 cup bean sprouts
3 scallions, green tops only,
chopped

SEASONINGS:
1 Tablespoon soy sauce
½ teaspoon sesame oil

COOK:
1. Heat the broth to a boil and then simmer the mushrooms for 5 minutes.
2. Add the bean curd and simmer 2 minutes.
3. Stir in the bean sprouts, scallions, soy sauce and sesame oil.

Serves 6.

PERFECT BOILED RICE

An essential part of every Chinese meal.

INGREDIENTS:
1 cup rice (well washed)
2 cups water

SEASONINGS:
1½ teaspoon salt

COOK:
1. Bring the water and salt to a boil. Add the rice and return to a boil.
2. Stir, then cover the saucepan and simmer for 20 minutes.
3. Uncover, stir again, and serve in a warmed dish.

ALMOND FRIED RICE

This recipe would be a compliment to either duck or chicken dishes.

INGREDIENTS:
4 cups cooked rice
1 cup blanched, slivered
　　almonds
¾ cup chopped fresh mush-
　　rooms
2 scallions, chopped
2 eggs, well beaten
3 Tablespoons oil

SEASONINGS:
1 clove garlic, cut in half
2 Tablespoons soy sauce

WOKCOOK:
　1. Heat the wok. Add 2 Tablespoons oil and the garlic, cooking for 15 seconds. Discard the garlic.
　2. Cook the eggs in the oil. Stir by turning them over gently. Remove the eggs from the pan and set aside.
　3. Add the last Tablespoon of oil to the wok. Stir-fry the mushrooms until they are soft. Add the rice. Heat and add the eggs, scallions, almonds and soy. Cook for 1 minute more and serve.

　Serves 6.

BEEF CONGEE

If rice is cooked for a long time with plenty of water, a thick Chinese porridge is formed. This is Congee.

INGREDIENTS:
1 cup rice, washed well and drained
3 quarts of water
2 cups beef broth
1 scallion, chopped
2 cups beef, shredded

SEASONINGS:
1 Tablespoon soy sauce
1 teaspoon sugar
½ teaspoon sesame oil
salt and pepper

COOK:
1. Marinate the beef shreds in the soy sauce.
2. Bring the rice and water to a boil in a large saucepan. Cover and simmer for 1½ hours without stirring.
3. Add the two cups broth and sugar, bringing it to a boil. Stir in the beef and when the rice again boils turn down the heat.
4. Simmer for 15 minutes more. Stir in the chopped scallions, sesame oil, salt and pepper.

Serves 6.

SHRIMP WITH ONIONS IN BLACK BEAN SAUCE

INGREDIENTS:
1 pound shrimp (medium sized), peeled and deveined
3 onions, cubed
1½ cups oil

SEASONINGS:
1 Tablespoon ginger, minced
3 cloves garlic, minced
2 Tablespoons fermented black beans soaked in boiling water 20 minutes and mashed in the sherry.
2 Tablespoons sherry
1 teaspoon sugar
MARINADE:
1 egg white
2 teaspoons cornstarch

WOKCOOK:

1. Marinate the shrimp for 15 mintues.
2. Heat the wok with the oil. Add the shrimp and shallow-fry for 2-3 minutes, until they are done. Drain in a seive-lined bowl.
3. Put 2 Tablespoons oil back into the wok. Stir-fry the bean mixture for 15 seconds and add the oinions, garlic, and ginger.
4. Stir-fry this until the edges of the onions become transparant.
5. Add the shrimp and the sugar, stirring until it is piping hot.
6. Serve immediately garnished with carrot shreds or parsley.

Shallow frying uses a slightly lower heat; however, when the cool shrimp are introduced, the oil temperature drops and the heat must be increased. To stir-fry the onions, a high heat and rapid, continuous stirring are required. All ingredients and seasonings must be at hand.

Serves 4 to 6.

SHRIMP WITH SNOW PEAS

INGREDIENTS:
1 pound medium shrimp,
    peeled and deveined
1½ cups snow peas, stems and
    strings removed
¼ cup oil

SEASONINGS
3 thin slices ginger, minced
2 cloves garlic, minced

SAUCE:
2 teaspoons sherry
½ teaspoon sugar
3 Tablespoons catsup
1½ Tablespoons soy sauce
¼ cup chicken broth
1 teaspoon cornstarch

WOKCOOK:

1. Heat the wok and add the oil. Stir-fry the snow peas for 1 minute and remove them from the wok.

2. Add the ginger and garlic to the hot wok and stir a few seconds.

3. Add the shrimp and stir-fry until the shrimp turn pink.

4. Mix the sauce and add it to the wok. When it is slightly thickened, return the snow peas to the wok, heat and serve.

Serves 4 to 6.

STEAMED FISH

INGREDIENTS:
1 whole fish, 2-3 lbs., cleaned, scaled and score-cut on both sides
2 cups shredded lettuce
2 scallions, chopped

SEASONINGS:
2 thin slices ginger, minced
1 garlic clove, crushed
2 Tablespoons fermented black beans soaked 20 minutes and crushed
½ teaspoon hot oil
3 Tablespoons soy sauce
1 Tablespoon sherry
½ teaspoon sugar

WOKCOOK:
1. Mix all the seasonings.
2. Rub the fish inside and out with the seasoning mix.
3. Place the whole fish in a shallow heat proof dish and place it in a steamer. Steam for 30 to 40 minutes until the fish is done.
4. Toss the lettuce shreds with the chopped scallions. Use this mixture to spread around the fish as a garnish. The lettuce will wilt slightly.

Serves 6.

STIR FRIED CHICKEN WITH BEAN SPROUTS

The bean sprouts should be crunchy and uncooked for an interesting contrast to the chicken and smooth sauce. Remember, when you stir-fry, it must be continuously. All ingredients and seasonings must be at hand.

INGREDIENTS:
2 whole chicken breasts, skinned, boned, and shredded
¼ cup Smithfield ham, shredded
¼ cup snow peas
2 cups bean sprouts
1 cup oil

SEASONINGS:
2 slices ginger, minced
1 clove garlic, crushed
½ teaspoon sesame oil
salt and pepper to taste

MARINADE:
1 Tablespoon dry sherry
1 egg white
2 Tablespoons cornstarch

SAUCE:
1 Tablespoon dry sherry
½ cup broth
½ teaspoon sugar
3 teaspoons cornstarch

47

WOKCOOK:

1. Mix the chicken with the marinade and refrigerate it for several hours.

2. Heat the wok to medium high heat, add 1 cup oil and stir-fry the chicken until it looses the pink color.

3. Drain the chicken and place it on a warmed platter.

4. Heat the wok and add 2 Tablespoons oil. When it begins to smoke, add the ginger and garlic, stir-frying a few seconds.

5. Add the peas and ham and continue to stir-fry for 1 minute.

6. Mix the sherry, sugar, 3 teaspoons cornstarch and ½ cup broth.

7. Add this sauce to the wok. Stir until it is slightly thickened. Return the chicken to the wok and add the bean sprouts, salt, and pepper. Stir this mixture for a few seconds. Sprinkle with sesame oil, season, and serve immediately.

Serves 6.

RED-STEW CHICKEN

INGREDIENTS:
4 to 6 pound stewing hen, cleaned, towel dried and loose fat removed
3 cups boiling water

SEASONINGS:
4 slices ginger
2 Tablespoons sherry
⅓ cup soy sauce
2 teaspoons honey

COOK:

1. Place the hen in a dutch oven with the boiling water.

2. After the mixture comes to a boil, add all seasonings and return it to a boil

3. Reduce the heat, cover and simmer for 2 hours, or until it it done.

4. Serve the chicken with boiled white steamed rice, and the cooking sauce (skim off the fat).

Serves 6.

BEEF WITH ONIONS

INGREDIENTS:
1½ pound beef steak cut in
    thin strips ¼ x ½ x 2
    inches
1½ cups onions cut in
    ¾ inch chunks
1 Tablespoon cornstarch
¼ cup beef broth
2 Tablespoons oil

SEASONINGS:
2 slices ginger, minced
1 clove garlic, crushed
salt and pepper

MARINADE:
3 Tablespoons soy sauce
1 Tablespoon sherry
½ teaspoon sugar

WOKCOOK:

1. Marinate the beef for 15 to 30 minutes.
2. Heat the wok on high heat. Add the oil. When it begins to smoke, add the ginger and garlic, stirring for a few seconds.
3. Add the onions and stir-fry to separate them. Cook the onions until they are somewhat transparent.
4. Remove the onions and add the beef to the wok. Stir-fry the beef until it loses its pink color and return the onions to the wok.
5. Dissolve the cornstarch in the broth. Add it to the beef.
6. When it is slightly thickened, return the onions to the wok.

Serve immediately garnished with parsley or watercress.

Serves 6.

STIR-FRIED BEEF AND PEPPERS

INGREDIENTS:
1 pound lean beef steak,
  thinly sliced
1 sweet red pepper, seeded,
  cut in ¾-inch squares
1 sweet green pepper, seeded,
  cut in ¾-inch squares
1 tomato, cut in wedges
4 Tablespoons oil

MARINADE:
2 garlic cloves, minced
1 onion, chopped
3 Tablespoons soy sauce
1 teaspoon cornstarch
1 Tablespoon oil

WOKCOOK:

1. Marinate the beef in the garlic, onion, soy sauce, cornstarch and oil for 15 to 30 minutes.

2. Heat the wok and add 2 Tablespoons oil. When it begins to smoke add the pepper and the tomatoes. Stir-fry until they are slightly softened and remove them from the wok.

3. Add the remaining oil. Drain the beef reserving the marinade. Stir-fry the beef in the wok until it begins to brown.

4. Return the peppers and tomato to the wok. Add the marinade and cook for 1 minute.

Serve immediately. Serves 6.

HOISIN PORK

INGREDIENTS:
1 pound pork, thinly sliced
  and shredded
1 teaspoon cornstarch
2 scallions, chopped
½ cup oil

SEASONINGS:
4 thin slices ginger, minced
1½ Tablespoons hoisin sauce
1 Tablespoon sherry
1 teaspoon sugar
1 Tablespoon soy sauce
½ teaspoon salt

WOKCOOK:

1. Mix the pork with the cornstarch.

2. Heat the oil in the wok. Stir-fry the pork shreds until they are well done. Remove the pork from the wok and drain it into a seive-lined bowl.

3. Put 1 Tablespoon oil in the wok. Add the ginger, hoisin sauce, and scallions. Heat thoroughly and add the remaining seasonings and the pork.

4. Cook for 1 minute more and serve immediately.

Garnish with Chinese Parsley.

Serves 4.

PORK WITH CASHEW NUTS

INGREDIENTS:
1 pound pork loin, thinly
   sliced
1 cup broccoli florets
1 carrot, shredded
3 scallions, split and cut in
   1-inch segments
½ cup bamboo shoots,
   thin-sliced and cut in
   ½-inch strips
1 cup unsalted roasted
   cashew nuts
4 Tablespoons oil

SEASONINGS:
2 slices ginger, minced
1 clove garlic, minced

MARINADE:
2 teaspoons soy sauce
2 teaspoons sherry
2 teaspoons cornstarch

SAUCE:
1 Tablespoon soy sauce
1 teaspoon cornstarch
½ teaspoon sugar

WOKCOOK:

1. Marinate the pork slices.
2. Heat the wok and add 2 Tablespoons of the oil.
3 When the oil begins to smoke add the ginger and garlic, stirring only a few seconds.
4. Add the broccoli and carrots. Stir-fry for 1 minute and add the bamboo shoots. Stir-fry briefly, and then lower the heat slightly. Cover the wok and cook the vegetables for 2 minutes. Then remove them from the wok.
5. Add the remaining 2 Tablespoons oil to the wok. Again turn the heat to high and stir-fry the pork until it loses its pink color.
6. Return the vegetables to the wok, adding the mixed sauce and the scallions. Stir until it is thickened.
7. Mix in the cashew nuts and serve.

Serves 6.

STIR-FRIED SPINACH WITH BACON

This recipe requires a large wok and rapid stirring.

INGREDIENTS:
1½ pounds fresh spinach
 leaves, washed and stems
 removed
6 bacon slices, cut into 1 inch
 pieces
3 scallions, chopped
4 fresh mushrooms, thinly
 sliced
2 Tablespoons oil

SAUCE:
1 Tablespoon vinegar
1 Tablespoon sherry
1 teaspoon sugar
¼ teaspoon dry mustard
2 teaspoons soy

WOKCOOK:

1. Heat the wok. Add the bacon and cook until almost crisp. Pour off the bacon grease.

2. Add 2 Tablespoons oil, the scallions, and fresh spinach. Stir-fry quickly until the volume of the spinach is reduced to one half.

3. Add the remaining ingredient with the sauce and cook 1 minute more.

Serve immediately. Serves 6.

BROCCOLI STEMS WITH SOY SAUCE

INGREDIENTS:
4 cups broccoli stems
  (florets removed), cut into
  $^3/_8$-inch slices. (cut across
  the stem)
4 Tablespoons oil

SEASONINGS:
2 Tablespoons soy sauce
1 teaspoon sherry
1 Tablespoon sugar

WOKCOOK:

1. Heat the wok and add the oil. When it begins to smoke add the broccoli and stir-fry for 1 minute.

2. Cover and cook for 10 minutes, stir in the seasonings, then simmer for 5 minutes more.

Serves 6.

BRAISED CHINESE CABBAGE

INGREDIENTS:
1 large head of Chinese
    Cabbage, sliced across in
    1-inch segments
2 scallions, chopped in
    1-inch pieces
3 Tablespoons oil

SEASONINGS:
1 clove garlic, minced
4 Tablespoons soy sauce
2 Tablespoons sherry
1 teaspoon sugar

WOKCOOK:
1. Heat the wok and add the oil. When it begins to smoke, add the garlic.

2. In a few seconds add the cabbage and scallions, stir-frying until the cabbage begins to soften (2 to 3 minutes).

3. Add the remaining seasonings and stir-fry for 2 minutes more.

Serve immediately on a heated platter.

Serves 4.

STIR-FRIED STRING BEANS

INGREDIENTS:
2 pounds string beans:
    remove the ends, cut in
    2 inch pieces, and dry
    thoroughly
2 dried black mushrooms
    soaked in boiling water for
    15 minutes, stems removed
    and thinly sliced
½ cup chicken broth
1 Tablespoon cornstarch
⅓ cup oil

SEASONINGS:
1 garlic clove, minced
3 Tablespoons sherry
2 teaspoons sugar
2 Tablespoons soy sauce
1 pinch cayenne

WOKCOOK:

1. Heat the wok and add the oil. When it begins to smoke fry the garlic for 30 seconds.

2. Add the string beans and mushrooms cooking until the beans turn a darker green.

3. Add the remaining seasonings and cook covered for 2 minutes.

4. Dissolve the cornstarch in the broth and add to the beans.

5. Stir-fry until the sauce has thickened.

Serves 6.

SWEET AND SOUR CARROTS

INGREDIENTS
4 cups carrots cut in match
   stick size slivers or cut into
   1/8 inch slices
2 scallions split and cut into
   1-inch pieces
2 Tablespoons oil

SEASONINGS:
1 thin slice ginger, minced
1 clove garlic, crushed

SAUCE:
1¼ cup water
¼ cup sugar
¼ cup brown sugar
1/3 cup red wine vinegar
1 Tablespoon soy sauce
2 Tablespoons cornstarch

WOKCOOK:

1. In a sauce pan, mix all of the sauce ingredients and heat until it starts to boil. Turn off the heat.

2. Heat the wok and add the oil, ginger and garlic. Stir-fry for 1 minute.

3. Reduce the heat and add the carrots, cooking them covered for 1 minute.

4. Add the scallions and the sauce. Bring the mixture to a boil and serve immediately.

Serves 6.

BEEF LO MEIN

The Chinese version of spaghetti!

INGREDIENTS:
½ pound beef steak, thinly
  sliced and shredded
½ pound fresh Chinese
  noodles, softened in boiling
  water for 5 minutes, then
  drain thoroughly
½ cup bamboo shoots
4 black mushrooms soaked in
  boiling water for 20 to 30
  minutes
½ cup Chinese cabbage,
  shredded
½ cup chopped scallions
1 cup bean sprouts
1 cup oil

SEASONINGS:
2 Tablespoons oyster sauce
2½ teaspoons sesame oil
½ teaspoon sugar
3 Tablespoons soy sauce
⅓ cup broth

WOKCOOK:

1. Marinate the beef in the oyster sauce
2. Heat the wok and add 1 cup oil. When it begins to smoke add the beef and stir-fry for 1 minute. Remove the meat and drain.
3. Leave 2 Tablespoons of oil in the wok and stir-fry the bamboo shoots and mushrooms for 30 seconds. Then add the cabbage and sugar.
4. Add 2 Tablespoons more of oil and all the ingredients except the sesame oil, scallions, and bean sprouts. Heat, turning gently for 5 minutes.
5. Add the bean sprouts, scallions, and sesame oil. Heat 1 minute more in a medium-hot wok, and serve immediately.

Serves 6-8.

SZECHWANESE PORK WITH VERMICELLI

Very spicy, this delicious dish is sometimes called, "ants climbing a tree."

INGREDIENTS:
¼ pound vermicelli soaked in warm water for 10 minutes and drain
½ pound pork, finely chopped
¼ cup sweet red pepper, finely shredded
1 cup broth
4 scallions, chopped
1 cup bean sprouts
1 Tablespoon oil

SEASONINGS:
1 Tablespoon ginger, finely chopped
2 garlic cloves, crushed
2 Tablespoons hot bean sauce
2 Tablespoons sherry
1 teaspoon sugar
2 Tablespoons soy sauce

WOKCOOK:

1. Heat the wok. Add 1 Tablespoon oil and the pork. Stir-fry until the pork looses all pink color, and breaks into tiny pieces.

2. Add the ginger, crushed garlic, and bean sauce. Stir-fry for 1 to 2 minutes and add the sweet red pepper. (Keeping a few shreds aside to garnish)

3. After stirring the red pepper into the pork mixture, add the remaining seasonings, plus the broth, and vermicelli.

4. Turn the heat to low and cook until the liquid is absorbed.

5. Toss with the scallions and beansprouts and serve.

Garnish with the remaining red pepper shreds.

Serves 6.

ALMOND TEA

INGREDIENTS
1½ cup blanched almonds
1 cup sugar
½ cup uncooked rice, washed
   thoroughly and soaked in
   boiling water for 1 hour
4 cups water

SEASONINGS
½ teaspoon almond extract

COOK:

1. Put the almonds and rice in the blender to grind with 1 cup water.

2. Strain the mixture through a cloth to use only the liquid. (Discard the almonds and rice.)

3. Cook this mixture in 4 cups water, stirring until it boils.

4. Add the sugar and return to a boil.

Serve hot. Serves 4.

8. EASY MEALS

Now we get to the fun part — preparing these dishes for guests. To make your planning easier, we've separated these easy meals into appropriate menus for two, four and six people. Great care has been taken to assure that tastes, textures and colors will blend perfectly, insuring a pleasing balance to these meals.

MENUS FOR TWO

1.

Subgum Vegetable Soup
Spinach with Pine Nuts
Spicy Ginger Duck
Scallion Foo Yong
Rice

SUBGUM VEGETABLE SOUP

INGREDIENTS:
1 chicken breast
¼ cup bamboo shoots cut
   into ¼-inch cubes
6-8 water chestnuts cut into
   ¼-inch cubes
1 stalk celery thin-sliced
1 cup snow peas, shredded
2 scallions, chopped
1 carrot cut in ¼-inch cubes
4 cups chicken broth

SEASONINGS:
1 Tablespoon soy sauce

COOK:

1. Bring the broth with the chicken breast to a boil. Reduce the heat and simmer for 20 minutes.

2. Remove the chicken from the bone and cut it in ½-inch cubes.

3. Put the chicken back in the broth with the vegetables and soy sauce. Simmer it for 10 minutes more and serve.

SPINACH WITH PINE NUTS

INGREDIENTS:
1 pound fresh spinach, rinse and drain well, remove stems
2 Tablespoons pine nuts toasted very lightly
2 Tablespoons oil

SEASONINGS:
2 teaspoons rice wine or sherry
1 teaspoon sugar
1 Tablespoon soy sauce

WOKCOOK:

1. Heat oil in wok and add spinach.

2. Stir-fry until half the volume, then add the seasonings and stir for 1 minute.

3. Remove from the wok with a slotted spoon and serve on a warmed platter. Sprinkle with the toasted pine nuts.

SPICY GINGER DUCK

INGREDIENTS:
4-5 pound duck, skinned,
boned and cut in very thin
slices. Mix with 1 Table-
spoon cornstarch
2 Tablespoons cornstarch
10-12 waterchestnuts, sliced
1 sweet red pepper, cut in
½-inch pieces
4 scallion stalks, chopped
¼ cup shredded carrots
2 cups oil

SEASONINGS:
¼ cup thinly sliced ginger
1 clove garlic, crushed

SAUCE:
2 Tablespoons sherry
1 teaspoon sugar
3 Tablespoons soy sauce
2 teaspoons vinegar
½ teaspoon sesame oil
¾ cup chicken broth
2 teaspoons "hot oil"
salt

WOKCOOK:
1. Heat the oil in a wok. Add the duck shreds. Shallow-fry for 2 minutes. Drain in a seive-lined bowl, leaving 1 Tablespoon oil in the wok.

2. Add the waterchestnuts and sweet red peppers, stir-fry for 1 minute and drain in the seive-lined bowl.

3. Put the "hot oil" in the empty wok. Add the ginger and scallions. Stir a few seconds. Blend the cornstarch with the sauce, and add this to the wok. Stir until thickened and add the cooked vegetables, sesame oil, and duck shreds. Heat until boiling.

4. Garnish with shredded carrots. Serve immediately.

SCALLION FOO YOUNG

INGREDIENTS:
2 eggs
1⅓ cups flour
⅔ cup thin sliced scallions
6 strips bacon, minced
1 cup chicken broth
¼ cup oil

SAUCE:
⅓ cup red wine vinegar
½ cup brown sugar
2 Tablespoons cornstarch
1 Tablespoon soy sauce
1 cup water

COOK:
1. Mix together eggs, flour, scallions, bacon, and broth.
2. Heat 1 Tablespoon oil in the skillet on medium-high heat.
3. Place ¼ of the mixture in the skillet and spread it out with a spatula. Cook until golden then turn it over.
4. Cook remaining batter in this manner. Serve it with sweet and sour sauce on the side.

THE SAUCE:
1. For the sweet and sour sauce, heat the water and brown sugar in a saucepan until the sugar is dissolved.
2. Dissolve cornstarch in the vinegar and soy and add to the sugar-water mixture. Heat until the cornstarch dissolves and the mixture thickens.

2.

Szechwan Cabbage and Pork Soup
Moo Goo Gai Pan
Deep-Fried Shrimp
Rice

SZECHWAN CABBAGE
AND PORK SOUP

The spicy Szechwan cabbage flavors this tasty soup.

INGREDIENTS:
½ pound pork, thinly sliced
  and shredded
⅓ cup bamboo shoots thinly
  sliced and cut into ½-inch
  strips
4 black mushrooms, pre-
  soaked and thinly sliced
⅓ cup Szechwan cabbage,
  shredded
8 snow peas, shredded lengthwise for garnish
4 cups broth
2 Tablespoons oil

SEASONINGS:
2 teaspoons soy sauce
1 Tablespoon sherry
salt to taste

MARINADE:
1 teaspoon cornstarch
2 teaspoons soy sauce

WOKCOOK:

1. Mix the pork with the marinade and let it stand for 15 to 30 minutes.

2. Heat the wok, add the oil and then the pork. Stir-fry until the pork is done, about 2 minutes.

3. Add the bamboo shoots, mushrooms, and cabbage. Stir for 1 minute and add the broth, soy sauce and sherry. Bring the soup to a boil.

Serve garnished with the snow peas.

63

MOO GOO GAI PAN

INGREDIENTS:
2 cups chicken breasts, cut
    into ½-inch cubes
1 Tablespoon cornstarch
2 cups bok choy hearts
8 ounces drained straw mush-
    rooms or canned button
    mushrooms
½ cup bamboo shoots, sliced
    to matchstick size
6 water chestnuts
½ cup snow peas
1 cup oil

SEASONINGS:
1 clove garlic
2 slices ginger, chopped
2 Tablespoons sherry

MARINADE:
1 Tablespoon cornstarch
1 egg white

SAUCE:
1 Tablespoon cornstarch
½ cup chicken broth
1 teaspoon sugar

WOKCOOK:

1. Marinate the chicken for 30 to 60 minutes.

2. Heat the wok and add the oil. Add the chicken, cooking it until it loses its pink color.

3. Remove the chicken from the wok with a seive and drain all but 2 Tablespoons of oil.

4. Heat the wok and add the garlic and ginger, stirring for 30 seconds.

5. Add the bok choy, mushrooms, bamboo shoots, water chestnuts, and snow peas. Stir-fry for 2 minutes.

6. Add the sherry. Cover and steam for 1 minute.

7. Return the chicken to the wok.

8. Mix the sauce ingredients and add to the wok. Cook, stirring, for 2 minutes and serve.

DEEP FRIED SHRIMP

INGREDIENTS:
1 pound shrimp, peeled and
    deveined
½ bunch scallions split length-
    wise and cut in half
Oil for deep frying

MARINADE:
2 cloves garlic, minced
2 Tablespoons sherry
1 teaspoon sugar
3 Tablespoons cornstarch
2 Tablespoons soy sauce

SAUCE:
¼ cup vinegar
2 Tablespoons ketchup
2 Tablespoons sugar
1 teaspoon worcestershire
    sauce

WOKCOOK:
1. Mix the shrimp with the marinade and let it stand for 1 hour.

2. Drain the shrimp well.

3. Heat a large wok with the oil for deep-frying until it is medium hot.

4. Deep-fry the shrimp stirring gently to separate.

5. When cooked (timing depends on the size of the shrimp), drain in a seive-lined bowl.

6. Combine the sauce ingredients in a pan with the scallions and bring to a boil.

7. Arrange the shrimp in a bowl. Drizzle the scallions and sauce on top.

3.

Shrimp Ball Soup
Snow Peas with Straw Mushrooms
Hot and Spicy Beef
Rice

SHRIMP BALL SOUP

INGREDIENTS:
1 pound shrimp, peeled and
deveined
4 egg whites
2 Tablespoons cornstarch
4 cups chicken broth
¼ cup watercress, stems
removed

SEASONINGS:
salt and pepper
hot oil to taste

COOK:
1. Mix the shrimp, egg whites, and cornstarch. Blend in an electric blender.
2. Form the shrimp balls in a wet spoon and drop them into boiling water. Return the water to a boil slowly.
3. Continue to boil the shrimp until they float.
4. With a slotted spoon, remove the shrimp from the water and place them in boiling broth.
5. Add watercress and the seasonings.

SNOW PEAS WITH STRAW MUSHROOMS

INGREDIENTS:
1 pound snow peas, stems and
strings removed
1 cup drained straw mush-
rooms
2 Tablespoons oil

SEASONINGS:
2 Tablespoons sherry
1 teaspoon sugar
1 teaspoon soy sauce
salt and pepper

66

WOKCOOK:

1. Heat the wok and add the oil. When it begins to smoke, add the snow peas and straw mushrooms.

2. Stir-fry for 2 minutes, then add the seasonings.

3. Stir for 1 minute more and serve immediately.

HOT AND SPICY BEEF

Delicious Szechwan style beef dish.

INGREDIENTS:
1 flank steak cut into very
   thin shreds
1 cup carrot shreds (size of
   match sticks)
1 cup celery, shredded (size
   of match sticks)
4-6 fresh hot peppers
1 cup oil

SEASONINGS:
4 slices ginger, minced
4 cloves garlic, minced
2 Tablespoons dark soy sauce
2 Tablespoons sherry
1 teaspoon sugar
1 teaspoon crushed hot red
   pepper

WOKCOOK:

1. Heat the wok and add the oil. When it begins to smoke, add the ginger and garlic. Cook 30 seconds, then add the beef.

2. Stir-fry the beef until it is browned and drain in a seive-lined bowl.

3. Heat 1 Tablespoon of the oil in the wok and add the carrots, celery, and pepper shreds. Stir-fry 1 minute.

4. Add remaining seasonings and the beef. Stir-fry 2 minutes more.

5. Serve with steamed white rice.

4.

WON TON SOUP (See page 83 for Won Ton recipe.)

INGREDIENTS:
4 cups chicken broth
1 cup spinach cut in 1 inch
    pieces
12 won ton
shredded ham or roast pork
1 Tablespoon oil

SEASONINGS:
salt and pepper
1 teaspoon sesame oil

WOKCOOK:

    1. Heat the wok and add 1 Tablespoon oil.

    2. Stir-fry the won ton for 1 minute, add the spinach, stir briefly and add the chicken broth, salt, pepper and sesame oil.

    3. Heat to boiling and garnish with the shredded ham or roast pork.

SHREDDED LAMB WITH ONIONS

INGREDIENTS:
1½ cups lamb (leg or shoulder)
    shredded
¼ cup bamboo shoots cut to
    matchstick size
4 onions cut to ¾ inch pieces
½ cup oil

SEASONINGS:
1 clove garlic, crushed

SAUCE:
1 Tablespoon soy sauce
1 Tablespoon sherry
¼ teaspoon salt
1 Tablespoon cornstarch
½ cup chicken broth

68

WOKCOOK:

1. Heat the wok and add the oil. When it begins to smoke, add the garlic. Thirty-seconds later, add the lamb and stir-fry until it loses its pink color. Remove from the wok, leaving 1 Tablespoon oil.

2. Stir-fry the onions and bamboo shoots 1 minute, Mix the sauce and add it to the wok, stirring until it is slightly thickened.

3. Return the lamb to the wok, heat thoroughly and serve.

Garnish with Chinese parsley.

STIR-FRIED ASPARAGUS TIPS

INGREDIENTS:
1 pound asparagus, roll-cut
  into 1 to 1½ inch segments.
  Remove bottom half and
  parboil the cut tops
1 sweet red pepper cubed
½ cup bamboo shoots, sliced
  and shredded to the size of
  matchsticks
2 Tablespoons oil.

SEASONINGS:
¼ cup broth
½ teaspoon salt
½ teaspoon sugar

WOKCOOK:

1. Heat the wok and add the oil.

2. When the oil begins to smoke, add the asparagus tips. Stir-fry for 1 minute and add the red peppers and bamboo shoots.

3. Stir-fry for one minute longer and add the broth with the seasonings.

4. Heat for 30 seconds longer and serve.

MENUS FOR FOUR

1.

Fuzzy Melon Soup
Lettuce Rolls with Fried Wild Rice
Exotic Chicken Salad
Crab Foo Yong
Rice

FUZZY MELON SOUP

INGREDIENTS:
¾ pound fuzzy melon, peeled
   and cut into ½ inch cubes
¼ pound pork, shredded
¼ pound tiny shrimp, peeled
   and deveined
4 cups broth
2 Tablespoons oil

SEASONINGS:
2 slices ginger minced
½ teaspoon sugar
1 Tablespoon soy sauce

WOKCOOK:

1. Heat the wok and add 1 tablespoon oil. When it begins to smoke, add the pork. Stir-fry until it is done, 2 to 3 minutes.

2. Add the shrimp, fuzzy melon, and ginger. Stir-fry for 1 minute and add the broth and remaining seasonings.

3. Simmer for 20 minutes and serve.

LETTUCE ROLLS

INGREDIENTS:
½ cup bamboo shoots, sliced
   to the size of matchsticks
1½ cup snow peas sliced thinly,
   lengthwise
½ cup pork, sliced thinly
2 Tablespoons oil
Romaine lettuce, cut and
   arranged standing in a bowl.

SEASONINGS:
1 clove garlic, minced

MARINADE:
1 Tablespoon soy sauce
1 teaspoon dry sherry
1 teaspoon sugar

WOKCOOK:
1. Mix the pork with the marinade.
2. Heat the wok and add the oil. Add the garlic and stir for 30 seconds.
3. Add the pork and stir-fry until it is brown.
4. Add snow peas and bamboo shoots. Cook 3 minutes.
5. Serve immediately; have the guests put a spoon of this mixture on a lettuce leaf with wild rice. Roll the lettuce leaf around the mixture and rice.

FRIED WILD RICE

INGREDIENTS:
1½ cup wild rice, cooked
2 Tablespoons oil

SEASONINGS:
¼ cup chopped chives
1½ Tablespoons soy sauce
1 teaspoon sherry
¼ teaspoon hot oil

WOKCOOK:
1. Heat the oil in the wok until it begins to smoke. Add the rice and stir-fry for 2 minutes.
2. Add all the seasonings and continue stirring for 30 seconds.

EXOTIC CHICKEN SALAD

Can be prepared in advance to complete the meal.

INGREDIENTS:
1 pound chicken breasts,
   cubed in 1-inch pieces
¼ cup cornstarch
2 cups oil
shredded head of iceberg
   lettuce
2 scallions, sliced
1 cup watercress (cut in
   1 inch pieces)
1 celery, thinly sliced
1 carrot, shredded

MARINADE:
3 Tablespoons soy sauce
1 minced garlic clove
1 thin slice of ginger
1 teaspoon rice wine or
   sherry
1 teaspoon sugar

DRESSING:
1 teaspoon sesame oil
1 Tablespoon vinegar
2 Tablespoons sesame seeds
2 Tablespoons vegetable oil

COOK:

   1. Marinate the chicken for 30 minutes.
   2. Roll it in cornstarch and deep-fry until golden.
   3. Place cooled chicken on a tossed salad of lettuce, scallions, watercress, celery, and carrots, with sesame oil dressing.

CRAB FOO YONG

INGREDIENTS:
1 cup crabmeat, cooked and
   diced
1 bunch scallions, sliced
1 stalk very thinly-sliced celery
2 cups bean sprouts
6 eggs, well beaten
Oil for frying

SEASONINGS:
1 slice minced ginger
1 Tablespoon soy sauce

WOKCOOK:

1. Heat the wok, Add 1 Tablespoon oil. Stir-fry the ginger, scallions, and celery until translucent but crisp.

2. Put these ingredients in a mixing bowl with crabmeat, beansprouts, eggs, and soy sauce.

3. Heat a little oil in a skillet or wok. Place ¼ cup of crabmeat mixture into the skillet and cook on a medium-high heat until it is lightly browned.

2.

Three Color Soup
Szechwan Scallops
Stir-fried Watercress
Chicken in Lemon Sauce
Rice

THREE COLOR SOUP

INGREDIENTS:
1 bean curd cake cut into ½ inch cubes
¾ cup peas
1 tomato, seeded and cubed
2 eggs, lightly beaten
6 cups chicken broth

SEASONINGS:
salt to taste

COOK:

1. Heat the broth to a boil. Add the peas, tomatoes, and bean curd. Simmer for five minutes.

2. Add the egg in a slow stream, stirring slowly. Add salt to taste.

Garnish with shredded ham.

SZECHWAN SCALLOPS

INGREDIENTS:
1¼ pound scallops
3 scallions sliced in ¼ inch
   pieces
¾ cup diced sweet red peppers
¾ cup diced sweet green peppers
⅓ cup bamboo shoots
8 sliced water chestnuts
4 black mushrooms soaked in
   boiling water for 15 minutes
   and sliced
¼ cup chicken broth
½ cup oil

SEASONINGS:
4 sliced ginger, minced
1 large clove garlic, minced
4 Tablespoons soy sauce
¼ teaspoon hot oil
1 teaspoon sugar
3 Tablespoons sherry
1 teaspoon vinegar
½ teaspoon Szechwan chili
   paste
1 Tablespoon hoisin sauce

WOKCOOK:

1. Heat the wok and add the oil. When it starts to smoke, add the scallops. Stir-fry for 3 minutes and drain in a seive-lined bowl.

2. Add 1 Tablespoon oil, scallions, ginger, and garlic, and cook for 30 seconds.

3. Add the peppers, bamboo shoots, water chestnuts, and mushrooms. Stir-fry for 2 minutes.

4. Return the scallops to the wok and add the remaining ingredients.

5. Cook for 1 minute and serve.

Serves 4

STIR-FRIED WATERCRESS

INGREDIENTS:
4 bunches watercress, stems
  removed
2 Tablespoons oil

SEASONINGS:
2 cloves garlic, halved
1 Tablespoon dry sherry
1 teaspoon sugar
2 Tablespoons soy sauce

WOKCOOK:
1. Heat the wok and add the oil. When it begins to smoke, add the garlic and the watercress leaves, stir-frying for 2 minutes.
2. Add the other ingredients and heat for 30 seconds.
3. Serve immediately, garnished with small, unpeeled apple pieces.

Serves 4 to 6

CHICKEN IN LEMON SAUCE

INGREDIENTS:
2 whole chicken breasts cut
  into 1 inch chunks
2 eggs, lightly beaten
½ cup cornstarch
6 black mushrooms soaked in
  boiling water for 15 to 30
  minutes
1 shredded red hot pepper
¼ cup sugar
½ green pepper, cubed
1 carrot, shredded
¼ cup pineapple chunks

MARINADE:
1 Tablespoon gin or vodka
1 teaspoon salt
1 Tablespoon soy sauce

SAUCE:
1 Tablespoon grated lemon
  juice of 1 lemon
½ cup broth
1 Tablespoon vinegar
1 teaspoon soy sauce
¼ cup sugar
1 Tablespoon cornstarch

75

WOKCOOK:

1. Marinate the chicken cubes in the gin, salt, and soy.
2. Roll the chicken cubes in the egg and then in the cornstarch.
3. Deep-fry the chicken until it is golden. Place on a warmed platter.
4. Remove all but 1 Tablespoon of oil from the wok. On high heat, stir-fry the mushrooms, hot peppers, green peppers, carrots, and pineapple. Add the lemon rind, juice, sugar, vinegar, and cornstarch dissolved in the broth.
5. Cook until thickened and pour over the chicken.
6. Garnish with cucumber and lemon slices.

3.

Sizzling Rice Soup
Hot Chinese Vegetable Salad
Lobster Cantonese
Braised Pork
Rice

SIZZLING RICE SOUP

INGREDIENTS:
1 pound small shrimp, peeled
 and deveined
½ cup diced water chestnuuts
½ cup cooked peas
8 black mushrooms soaked in
 boiling water for 15 to 30
 minutes and sliced
3 scallions, chopped
6 cups chicken broth
2 Tablespoons oil

SEASONINGS:
¼ teaspoon hot oil
1 Tablespoon soy sauce

WOKCOOK:

1. Heat the wok. Add the oil and shrimp. Stir-fry 1 minute, then add the water chestnuts, peas, black mushrooms, and scallions.

2. Add the broth and seasonings. Bring to a boil and simmer for 5 minutes.

3. Prepare "sizzling rice" and put it into the soup at the table just before serving.

SIZZLING RICE

INGREDIENTS:
1½ cups rice
2 cups water
Oil for deep frying

SEASONINGS:
½ teaspoon salt

1. Wash the rice well. Put in a pan with the 2 cups water and bring to a boil. Boil uncovered for 10 minutes and simmer 20 minutes covered tightly.

2. Put the rice in a long rectangular metal pan and bake uncovered for 30 to 40 minutes. The rice will be dry enough to be removed from the pan and broken into squares.

3. Heat the oil for deep frying to a medium heat and fry the rice cakes until they are golden.

Serve immediately.

HOT CHINESE VEGETABLE SALAD

INGREDIENTS:
1 large green sweet pepper
1 large red sweet pepper
2 medium sized carrots
3 medium sized zucchini
All of the above are
   cut into shreds
3 scallions, split and cut into
   1½ inch segments
4 Tablespoons oil

SEASONINGS:
2 garlic cloves, minced
3 thin slices ginger, minced
4 Tablespoons soy sauce
1 teaspoon hot sauce or
   tabasco
2 Tablespoons sherry
2 teaspoons sugar
2 Tablespoons vinegar
1 Tablespoon sesame oil

WOKCOOK:
1. Heat the wok and add the oil. When it begins to smoke, add the ginger and garlic, stir-frying for 30 seconds.
2. Add all the ingredients except the sesame oil.
3. Stir-fry, turning the vegetables, for 2 minutes.
4. Add the sesame oil and cook for 1 minutes. Serve.

LOBSTER CANTONESE

INGREDIENTS:
3 lobster tails, tail-fins
   chopped off and remaining
   tail chopped in ½ inch slices
   (with shell if possible)
½ pound ground pork
⅓ cup bamboo shoots sliced
   in shreds the width of
   double matchsticks
1 cup snow peas, shredded
   lengthwise
2 scallions, chopped
2 eggs, beaten
2 Tablespoons oil
1½ cup chicken stock

SEASONINGS:
2 cloves garlic, minced
salt and pepper
1 Tablespoon soy
2 Tablespoons sherry
1 teaspoon sugar
¼ cup water
1 Tablespoon cornstarch
1 Tablespoon vinegar
   (optional)

78

WOKCOOK:

1. Heat the wok. Add the oil and garlic, stirring a few seconds.
2. Add the pork and lobster, stirring to separate the pork. Immediately add the chicken stock, soy, sherry, and sugar. Cover and cook over medium heat for 8 minutes.
3. Add the bamboo shoots and snow peas to the simmering meat. Cook for 2 minutes more.
4. Stir in the eggs in a slow stream, then add the scallions.
5. Mix the cornstarch and water and add to the wok. Stir until slightly thickened. Pull the lobster shells out. Salt and pepper to taste.

Serve immediately with steamed rice.

BRAISED PORK

INGREDIENTS:
3 pounds lean loin pork cut
   in ¾ inch cubes
¼ cup plus 2 teaspoons
   cornstarch
4 scallions cut in 1 inch
   pieces
2 cups bean sprouts
Oil for deep frying

SEASONINGS:
4 thin slices ginger
2 garlic cloves, crushed
1 teaspoon sugar
½ teaspoon Five Spice
   Powder
½ cup soy sauce
2 Tablespoons brandy
½ cup water

MARINADE:
2 Tablespoons soy sauce
1 Tablespoon brandy
½ teaspoon salt
¼ teaspoon pepper

WOKCOOK:

1. Cover pork with marinade and let stand for 30 minutes.
2. Drain the pork and toss with the cornstarch.
3. Heat the oil in a wok. Deep fry the coated pork until it is browned, a few pieces at a time. Drain and set aside.
4. Place 1 Tablespoon oil in the wok and fry the ginger and garlic for 15 seconds. Add the sugar, Five Spice Powder, soy sauce, brandy, ½ cup water and the pork.
5. Simmer for 2 hours, covered.
6. Stir-fry the scallions for 1 minute in 1 Tablespoon oil.
7. Pour 1 cup boiling water over the bean sprouts and drain after 1 minute.
8. Dissolve 2 teaspoons cornstarch in ¼ cup water and add to the simmering pork. Thicken and put in a shallow dish.
9. Mix the scallions and beansprouts and garnish the outer edge of the pork with this mixture.

4.

Shrimp Toast
Pork with Green Vegetable Soup
Beef with Broccoli
Fried Won Ton
Vegetables in Sweet and Sour Sauce
Rice

SHRIMP TOAST

INGREDIENTS:
1 pound shrimp, minced
1 large onion, minced
1 egg white, slightly beaten
2 eggs, beaten
1 cup breadcrumbs
Oil for deep frying
Thin bread cut in squares

SEASONINGS:
3 slices ginger, minced
½ teaspoon sugar

80

COOK:

1. Mix the shrimp, onion, egg whites, ginger, and sugar.
2. Dip the bread square in the beaten egg, then in the bread-crumbs.
3. Spread the shrimp mixture over the bread.
4. Again, dip it in the egg and breadcrumbs and deep-fry until it is golden.
5. Sprinkle with chopped parsley and serve.

PORK WITH GREEN VEGETABLE SOUP

INGREDIENTS:
1½ pounds spare-ribs halved
   and cut into individual ribs
½ cucumber cut into double
   matchstick size strips
1 cup bok choy hearts cut
   into shreds
2 scallions, chopped
6 cups chicken broth

SEASONINGS:
a few drops of "hot oil"

COOK:

1. Boil the spare ribs for 10 minutes in water. Discard the water.
2. Heat the broth and add the spareribs. Simmer for 1 hour, then add the vegetables.
3. Heat to a boil, add the "hot oil" and serve.

BEEF WITH BROCCOLI

INGREDIENTS:
1½ cups tender beef sliced in thin strips
4 black mushrooms soaked in boiling water for 15 minutes and sliced
2 cups broccoli thinly-sliced across the stalks, and the flower heads cut in small 1-inch pieces
½ cup broth
1 Tablespoon cornstarch
¼ cup oil

SEASONINGS:
2 Tablespoons soy sauce
2 cloves garlic, minced
2 thin slices of ginger, minced

WOKCOOK:
1. Mix the soy sauce with the beef.
2. Heat the oil in the wok and add the garlic and ginger, cooking for 30 seconds.
3. Add the beef and stir-fry until the beef loses the pink color. Drain the beef in a seive-lined bowl.
4. Heat 1 Tablespoon oil in the wok and add the broccoli and mushrooms. Stir-fry for 1 minute, add half the broth, and cover and cook for three minutes.
5. Return the beef to the wok and add the cornstarch dissolved in the remaining broth. Cook 1 minute until the sauce thickens and serve.

BASIC WON TON

INGREDIENTS:
1 cup ground pork
¼ pound shrimp peeled, de-
    veined, and finely minced
½ cup water chestnuts, finely
    chopped
2 scallions, minced
1 teaspoon cornstarch
1 package won ton skins

SEASONINGS:
1 teaspoon soy sauce
1 teaspoon sherry
½ teaspoon salt

THE FILLING:
Mix-well all ingredients and seasonings except the won ton skins.

TO FILL THE WON TONS: (See illustration on next page.)
1. Place won ton skins on a flat surface. Put 1 teaspoon of the filling one inch above the bottom corner. Fold the corner over twice (2/3 the height of the square.)
2. Put a very tiny dab of the filling on the top of the right hand corner.
3. Fold the left corner over the center.
4. Fold the right corner over the center and pinch firmly to seal.
5. As you work, cover the finished won tons with a damp cloth to keep them from drying.
6. Simmer them in the water until they float.

FRIED WON TON

Use the above recipe for Basic Won Ton

COOK:
1. Heat 3-4 cups oil to 350 degrees and fry 12 uncooked won tons for 5 to 8 minutes or until golden.
2. Serve with vegetables in sweet and sour sauce.

Serves 6-8

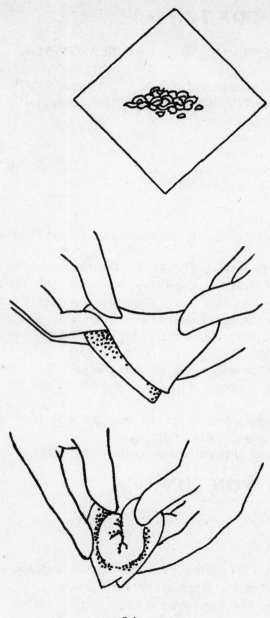

VEGETABLES IN SWEET AND SOUR SAUCE

INGREDIENTS:
1 medium green pepper, cubed
1 medium red pepper, cubed
1 large onion cut in ½ to ¾
    pieces (will separate as it
    is cooked)
1 carrot cut across in ¼ inch
    pieces
1 tomato, peeled, seeded,
    and cubed
½ cup pineapple chunks,
    drained
2 Tablespoons oil

SEASONINGS:
1 slice ginger, minced

SAUCE:
½ cup chicken broth
2 Tablespoons cornstarch
1 Tablespoon soy sauce
½ cup brown sugar
½ cup vinegar
1 teaspoon salt

WOKCOOK:
    1. Mix the cornstarch with the chicken broth in a saucepan.
    2. Add the soy, brown sugar, vinegar, and salt. Cook, stirring, until the sugar melts and the mixture thickens. Set aside.
    3. Heat the wok and add 2 Tablespoons oil.
    4. When the oil begins to smoke, add the ginger and cook for 15 seconds.
    5. Add all the vegetables and stir-fry until the onions separate and appear transparent at the edges, but crisp in the middle.
    6. Add the pineapple and sweet and sour sauce. Heat thoroughly and serve.

Serves 6

MENUS FOR SIX

1.

Rich Hot and Sour Soup
Szechwan Cabbage
Barbequed Shortribs
Duck with Tangerine
Bean Curd Homestyle
Rice

RICH HOT AND SOUR SOUP

An impressive favorite.

INGREDIENTS:
½ cup pork, shredded
6 dried tiger lily buds, pre-
   soaked in boiling water for
   15 minutes: cut these in
   half and remove hard ends
6 dried black mushrooms, pre-
   soaked for 15 minutes in
   boiling water: remove
   stems and slice thinly
½ cup shredded bamboo shoots
4 cups chicken broth
1 Tablespoon cornstarch
¼ cup water
1 pad fresh white beancurd,
   cut in ½" cubes
2 eggs, lightly beaten
¼ cup scallions, chopped
1 Tablespoon oil

SEASONINGS:
2 thin slices ginger, minced
1 clove garlic, crushed
1½ Tablespoons soy sauce
4 Tablespoons red wine
   vinegar
1 Tablespoon sesame oil
¼ teaspoon "hot oil"
salt and pepper

COOK:

1. Heat wok and add the oil, garlic, and ginger, stirring for 30 seconds.

2. Add the pork, cooking until it loses its pink color. Add the soy sauce and cook 1 minute more.

3. Then add bamboo shoots, mushrooms, and tiger lily stems and stir quickly 1 minute.

4. Stir in chicken broth and vinegar.

5. Combine the cornstarch and water and add to the simmering broth.

6. Add the beancurd and bring the soup to a boil.

7. Turn the heat on low, and add the scallions. Then add the beaten eggs in a slow stream, stirring several times.

8. Turn off heat and add the sesame and hot pepper oil. Season to taste and serve immediately.

SZECHWAN CABBAGE

INGREDIENTS:
½ head of a large firm Chinese cabbage cut into 1½ inch chunks
1 quart boiling water

SEASONINGS:
½ teaspoon salt
1 teaspoon Szechwan peppercorns
1 Tablespoon crushed dried red pepper
4 cloves garlic crushed
1 Tablespoon rice vinegar

WOKCOOK:

1. Heat the wok and place the peppercorns in the moderately hot wok to roast a few seconds only.

2. Put the salt in the boiling water and pour this over the cabbage that has been placed in a 2 quart jar. Add the peppercorns, crushed dried red peppers, garlic and vinegar.

3. Cover tightly and let stand for several days. It may be stored for 1½ to 2 weeks.

BARBEQUED SHORTRIBS

INGREDIENTS:
6 pounds shortribs cut into 2
 inch lengths. Slash the meat
 to the bone so that it is
 sectioned into ½ inch
 squares

SEASONINGS:
1 Tablespoon fresh ginger,
 minced
1 clove garlic, crushed
½ cup soy sauce
2 Tablespoons sugar
2 Tablespoons sesame oil

COOK:
  1. Mix the seasonings and heat them to boiling. Pour this over
the shortribs and let them marinate for 1 to 2 hours.
  2. Cook the shortribs over charcoal or if this is unavailable,
broil until done.

Garnish with scallion flowers.

Note: To make scallion flowers, cut the white and light green
parts of a scallion into 2 inch lengths. Then shred both ends of
the scallion piece leaving the shreds attached. Put the cut scallions in ice water and the feathered ends will curl.

DUCK WITH TANGERINE

INGREDIENTS:
3 to 4 pound duck cut
 into 8 to 10 pieces
½ cup plus 1 Tablespoon
 cornstarch
2 tangerines, peeled, halved,
Oil for deep-frying

SEASONINGS:
4 scallions, chopped
2 teaspoons ginger, minced
¼ cup boiling water
1 teaspoon salt
⅛ teaspoon pepper

SAUCE:

1 Tablespoon sugar
½ cup soy sauce
1 cup red wine
1 cup broth
Several long tangerine peels
1 cup tangerine juice

COOK:

1. Pour ¼ cup boiling water over the chopped scallions and ginger.

2. Coat the duck pieces with this liquid, salt, and pepper then let them stand for several hours.

3. Heat the oil in the wok. Lightly rub the duck pieces with cornstarch and deepfry for 4 to 5 minutes. Fry only a few pieces at a time.

4. Drain the duck.

5. Mix the ingredients for the sauce in a large saucepan. Bring it to a boil then add the fried duck and simmer for 45 minutes or until the duck is tender.

6. Meanwhile mix 1 Tablespoon cornstarch with 1/3 cup water and bring to a boil. Add the sliced tangerine and remove from the heat.

7. Place the duck and sauce in a shallow serving dish. Coat the duck with the glaze, using the sliced tangerines to decorate.

BEAN CURD HOMESTYLE

INGREDIENTS:
3 beancurd cakes, cut in 1
   inch cubes
½ pound pork loin, thin-
   sliced
4 black mushrooms, pre-
   soaked and sliced
2 Tablespoons cloud ears,
   presoaked and shredded
½ cup sliced bamboo shoots
3 scallions (green only)
Oil for deep frying

SEASONINGS:
3 slices ginger, finely minced
2 cloves garlic, crushed
1 Tablespoon hot bean sauce
1 teaspoon fermented black
   beans, soaked for 15
   minutes and crushed

SAUCE:
1 Tablespoon sherry
½ teaspoon sugar
3 Tablespoons soy sauce
1 Tablespoon cornstarch
1 cup broth

MARINADE:
1 teaspoon cornstarch
1 teaspoon soy sauce

WOKCOOK:
   1. Heat the oil for deep frying over medium heat.
   2. Deep fry the bean curd until golden. Remove and place gently on a warm platter.
   3. Turn the heat to high and deep-fry the pork until it is lightly browned. Remove and drain the pork.
   4. Pour off all but 1 Tablespoon oil. Add the ginger, garlic, mushrooms, cloud ears, bamboo shoots, scallions, black beans, bean sauce, and cooked pork. Stir-fry for 1 minute.
   5. Add the sauce. Stir until it is thickened, and return the beancurd to the wok.
   6. Stir gently until thoroughly heated.

Serve immediately.

2.

Chinese Mushroom Soup
Cucumber Cool
Twice-cooked Pork with Bitter Melon
Stir-fried Chicken with Almonds
Seven-spice Shrimp
Chow Mai Fon with Pork
Rice

CHINESE MUSHROOM SOUP

INGREDIENTS:
2 dried black mushrooms
½ pound fresh mushrooms
    chopped
6 cups chicken stock

SEASONINGS:
6 Tablespoons sherry
few drops "hot oil"

1. Pour boiling water to cover the dried mushrooms and let them stand for 3 to 4 hours.
2. Drain the liquid from the soaked mushrooms. Discard the mushrooms and put the liquid in a saucepan with the broth and chopped fresh mushrooms.
3. Simmer the soup for 10 minutes and strain it.
4. Add sherry and hot oil.

Garnish with a few thin slices of fresh mushrooms

CUCUMBER COOL

INGREDIENTS:
3 medium cucumbers, peeled, seeds removed, and cut in very thin slices
10 red radishes, sliced

SEASONINGS:
1 teaspoon salt
2 cloves garlic, crushed
2 teaspoons vinegar
1 Tablespoon soy sauce
1 teaspoon sugar
2 Tablespoons peanut oil

COOK:

1. Sprinkle salt over the cucumbers and let them stand for 30 minutes, then rinse and drain.

2. Mix 1 clove garlic, 1 teaspoon vinegar, 1 Tablespoon soy sauce, 1 teaspoon sugar, and 1 Tablespoon peanut oil. Toss with the cucumbers, and put them in a serving dish and sprinkle with fresh chopped parsley.

3. Mix the remaining garlic, vinegar, and peanut oil.

4. Just before serving, arrange the radishes in a border around the edge of the cucumbers in the dish and drizzle the garlic dressing over them.

TWICE-COOKED PORK
WITH BITTER MELON

INGREDIENTS:
2 pounds boned pork loin
3 scallions, chopped
3 cups hot water
1 small sweet green pepper, cubed
1 small sweet red pepper
½ cup bamboo shoots, cut to the size of a double matchsick
¾ cup bitter melon: discard center pulp and seeds, cut in ¼ inch slices and parboil
2 Tablespoons oil

SEASONINGS:
3 garlic cloves, crushed
3 slices ginger, minced
1 teaspoon crushed hot red pepper flakes
1 Tablespoon sherry
2 Tablespoons soy sauce
1 Tablespoon hoisin sauce

COOK:

1. Cook the pork with water and scallions in a covered saucepan and bring to a boil. Simmer covered for 1 hour.

2. Cool the meat and slice in ¼-inch strips, across the grain.

3. Heat the wok and add 2 Tablespoons oil. Cook the garlic for 30 seconds.

4. Stir-fry the pork strips, ginger, and hot red pepper until the pork is browned (2 to 3 minutes).

5. Add the sweet green and red peppers and stir-fry for 1 minute more.

6. Add the remaining ingredients and seasonings and stir-fry for 2 minutes.

STIR-FRIED CHICKEN WITH ALMONDS

INGREDIENTS:
2 whole chicken breasts, boned, skinned, and shredded

½ cup blanched, slivered almonds (roast for 5 minutes)

4 hot green chili peppers, shredded

1 small head Romaine lettuce, washed and dried

3 Tablespoons chicken stock

3 Tablespoons oil

SEASONINGS:
2 thin slices ginger, minced

MARINADE:
1 Tablespoon cornstarch

1 egg white

1 Tablespoon rice wine or sherry

1 teaspoon sugar

WOKBOOK:
1. Mix the chicken with the marinade.

2. Heat the wok, add 2 Tablespoons oil, and add the chili peppers. Cook 15 seconds and add ginger and chicken. Cook the chicken until it turns white. Then mix the cornstarch and chicken stock and add this to the chicken in the wok.

3. Thicken the sauce and mix in the almonds.

4. Serve with the lettuce. Place the lettuce in your hand and fill with chicken, folding the sides of the lettuce leaf over the filling.

SEVEN-SPICE SHRIMP

INGREDIENTS:
1 pound shrimp, peeled and
    deveined
1/3 cup sliced water chestnuts
1/3 cup bamboo shoots
6 slices bacon, chopped
1 Tablespoon cornstarch,
    dissolved
1 cup water
1 cup chopped scallions
1/2 cup oil

SEASONINGS:
1/3 cup ginger, minced
2 Tablespoons chopped garlic
1/2 teaspoon shredded hot
    pepper
2 Tablespoons soy sauce
2 teaspoons sugar

MARINADE:
2 teaspoons cornstarch
1 egg white

WOKCOOK:

1. Place the shrimp in the marinade for 30 minutes.

2. Heat the oil in the wok. Add the shrimp and stir-fry until they are pink.

3. Pour the shrimp and oil into a seive-lined bowl.

4. Fry the bacon until golden and pour this into the seive-lined bowl.

5. Add 1 Tablespoon oil to the wok. Stir-fry water chestnuts, bamboo shoots, ginger, garlic, and hot peppers for 1 minute.

6. Add soy sauce, sugar, shrimp and bacon. Dissolve 1 Tablespoon cornstarch in 1 cup of water. Add this to the shrimp mixture.

7. Bring to a boil; add scallions and stir until it is slightly thickened.

CHOW MAI FON WITH PORK

INGREDIENTS:
½ pound lean pork, cut in
    thin shreds
6 small black mushrooms,
    soaked in boiling water for
    15 minutes and sliced
2 cups bean sprouts, root ends
    removed
2 cups noodles, cooked
    2 minutes in 2 quarts of
    boiling water, then drained
1½ cups shredded celery cabbage
½ cup chives, chopped
2 Tablespoons chicken broth
4 Tablespoons oil

SEASONINGS:
1 clove garlic, crushed
1 Tablespoon dry sherry
2 Tablespoons soy sauce
½ teaspoon hot oil

WOKCOOK:

1. Heat the wok and add 2 Tablespoons oil. When it begins to smoke, add the garlic, stirring a few seconds.

2. Then stir-fry the pork until it loses the pink color. Add 1 Tablespoon soy sauce and cook 30 seconds.

3. Add the mushrooms and cabbage, cooking 30 seconds.

4. Add the noodles, chives, sherry, 1 Tablespoon soy sauce, and chicken broth. Cook three minutes, tossing lightly.

5. Add the bean sprouts and hot oil, mixing well.

3.

Preserved Vegetable and Noodle Soup
Aromatic Beef
Moo Shu Pork with Chinese Pancakes
Szechwan Fried String-beans
Chicken with Hoisin Sauce
Crab Lo Mein
Rice

PRESERVED VEGETABLE AND NOODLE SOUP

INGREDIENTS:
¼ pound pork, shredded
8 black mushrooms, soaked
  for 15 to 30 minutes and
  sliced
2 ounces cellophane noodles,
  soaked, drained, and cut a
  few times
¼ cup preserved vegetable,
  shredded
2 scallions, chopped
4 cups water
2 cups chicken broth

SEASONINGS:
1 teaspoon salt
½ teaspoon sesame oil

COOK:
1. Bring all the ingredients except the noodles, scallions and sesame oil to a boil and cook for 5 minutes.
2. Add the noodles and bring the soup to a boil again.
3. Add the scallions and sesame oil. Reduce the heat, cook for 1 minute more and serve.

AROMATIC BEEF

INGREDIENTS:
3 pounds shin of beef, bones
  removed
3 scallions, chopped
2 Tablespoons oil
1 cup watercress, stems
  removed

SEASONINGS:
2 garlic cloves, crushed
3 thin slices ginger
2 star anise seeds
$\frac{1}{3}$ cup soy sauce
¼ cup sherry
1 Tablespoon brown sugar
8 peppercorns
1 teaspoon sesame oil

WOKCOOK:
1. Heat the oil in a wok. Add the beef, garlic, and ginger. Brown all sides of the meat.

2. Add the remaining ingredients except the watercress. Cover the meat with boiling water and simmer for 2½ hours or until tender.

3. Put the beef in a dish, strain the liquid, and pour it over the beef.

4. Chill and cut into ¼-inch slices. Cube the jelly and serve with the slice beef rolls on a bed of watercress.

MOO SHU PORK

Chinese Pancakes (see recipe on following page)
  Make one recipe and start steaming them.

INGREDIENTS:
¾ cup bamboo shoots, cut
  into matchstick size shreds
20 dried tiger lily buds, cut in
  half and hard ends removed
4 cloud ear mushrooms, cover
  with boiling water for 15 to
  30 minutes, remove stems
  and slice
¼ cup plus 2 Tablespoons oil
¼ pound pork, shredded
4 eggs, lightly beaten
¼ cup chicken broth
1 cup thinly sliced bok choy
  hearts
4 scallions chopped

SEASONINGS:
1 clove garlic, minced
2 teaspoons soy sauce
½ teaspoon sugar
Hot oil

WOKCOOK:
  1. Heat 2 Tablespoons oil in a wok. When it begins to smoke, add the garlic, stirring a few seconds.
  2. Add the pork shreds and stir-fry until it loses the pink color. Then add soy sauce, bamboo shoots, tiger lily buds, and mushrooms.
  3. Stir-fry the pork with the vegetables for 1 minute and pour this mixture into seived-lined bowl.
  4. Place ¼ cup oil in the wok and heat.
  5. Scramble the eggs, gently turning them in the oil. Pour in the broth and heat.
  6. Add the sugar, bok choy, pork mixture, and scallions.
  7. Stir to mix and serve with the steamed pancakes and hot oil.

CHINESE PANCAKES

INGREDIENTS:
2 cups sifted all purpose flour
1 cup boiling water
1 Tablespoon sesame oil for cooking

COOK:
1. Pour the boiling water into the flour, slowly stirring to mix the dough.

2. Knead the dough until it is smooth and elastic. (Approximately 5 minutes)

3. On a lightly floured surface roll the dough with your hands into a long cylinder 18 inches long.

4. Cut into 1-inch pieces.

5. Dip one piece in sesame oil and put it against an unoiled piece.

6. Roll out both together to make a very thin 4-inch pancake.

7. Fry in a lightly oiled skillet on moderate heat until bubbles form. Flip to other side and cook but do not brown.

8. As you remove the pancake from the skillet pull them apart to make two. Keep them under a damp cloth until they have all been cooked.

9. When you are ready to serve them, put the pancakes in foil together and steam them for 10 minutes.

Fill with your favorite filling.

SZECHWAN FRIED STRING BEANS

INGREDIENTS:
1½ pounds string beans, stems
   removed, cut into 2-inch
   pieces; dried thoroughly
½ pound ground lean pork
2 cups oil

SEASONINGS:
1 clove garlic, minced
1 slice ginger, minced
2 teaspoons dried red pepper
   flakes
1 teaspoon sugar
1 Tablespoon sherry
1 Tablespoon soy sauce

WOKCOOK:

1. Heat the oil in the wok until it begins to smoke. Add the string beans and cook for 8 to 10 minutes.

2. Drain the beans and keep 1 Tablespoon of the oil in the wok.

3. Cook the garlic and ginger for 30 seconds.

4. Add the ground pork and red peppers and stir-fry until the pork is well done and the lumps have been broken up into very small bits.

5. Add the soy, sugar, sherry, and beans. Stir-fry for 1 minute and serve.

CHICKEN WITH HOISIN SAUCE

INGREDIENTS:
2 whole chicken breasts,
   skinned, boned, and cubed
   in ¾-inch pieces
1 sweet green pepper, cubed
8 water chestnuts, sliced
½ pound mushrooms, sliced
   thinly
½ cup cashew nuts
4 Tablespoons oil

SEASONINGS:
3 Tablespoons hoisin sauce

MARINADE:
1 Tablespoon sherry
1 Tablespoon soy sauce
1 Tablespoon cornstarch

WOKCOOK:

1. Marinate the chicken in the sherry, soy sauce, and cornstarch.

2. Heat the wok and add 1 Tablespoon oil. Stir-fry the green pepper, water chestnuts, and mushrooms for 2 minutes and remove from the wok.

3. Put the remaining 3 Tablespoons oil in the wok. Stir-fry the chicken until it is done, about 3 minutes.

4. Add the vegetables, hoisin sauce, and cashews. Stir, heat, and serve immediately.

CRAB LO MEIN

INGREDIENTS:
½ pound thin noodles cooked, rinsed and drained
1½ cups king crabmeat, cooked and thoroughly drained
¼ cup shredded roast pork or ham
6 black mushrooms soaked in boiling water for 15 to 30 minutes and sliced
1 cup green beans cut "French style"
1 cup bean sprouts
¼ cup scallions, chopped
3 Tablespoons oil

SEASONINGS:
1 clove garlic, minced
2 thin slices of ginger minced
3 Tablespoons soy sauce
½ teaspoon sesame oil

MARINADE:
1 Tablespoon sherry
1 teaspoon sugar

WOKCOOK:

1. Marinate the crabmeat in the sherry and sugar.

2. Heat the wok and add 2 Tablespoons oil. When it begins to smoke, add the garlic clove and ginger. Cook for a few seconds and add the green beans, mushrooms, and crabmeat. Cook out the liquid for 1 to 2 minutes.

3. Add the remaining ingredients and stir gently until the noodles are piping hot.

4.

Velvet Corn Soup with Crab Meat
Skewed Lamb
Chicken Cooked in Paper
Sesame Green Bean Salad
Eggplant in Garlic Sauce
Roast Pork with Black Bean Sauce
Rice

VELVET CORN SOUP WITH CRAB MEAT

INGREDIENTS:
1 cup canned crabmeat,
  washed and drained
6 cups chicken broth
2 cups sweet corn, cream style
2 eggs, separated; yolks lightly
  beaten, whites stiffly beaten

SEASONINGS:
¼ teaspoon salt
¼ teaspoon pepper

MARINADE:
1 slice ginger, minced
2 teaspoons cornstarch
1 Tablespoon sherry

WOKCOOK:

1. Marinate the crab meat in the ginger, sherry, and corn-starch.

2. Heat the chicken stock. Add the corn and bring it to a boil.

3. Add the crabmeat mixture and again bring to a boil.

4. Turn the heat down and gently stir in the egg yolks, then fold in the egg whites.

Garnish with chopped parsley.

SKEWED LAMB

INGREDIENTS:
1½ pound leg of lamb, cut
   in thinnest possible strips
   ⅛ x 1 x 3 inches

MARINADE:
2 cloves garlic, crushed
3 Tablespoons ginger, minced
¼ cup soy sauce
3 Tablespoons sherry
2 Tablespoons sugar
3 Tablespoons, sesame oil.

1. Marinate the lamb overnight.

2. String the lamb on the small skewers in an accordian effect, folding each 3-inch strip 3 times.

3. Brown under the broiler. Use a small flame device in the serving area. The guests reheat the meat and eat it with plum sauce and mustard.

CHICKEN COOKED IN PAPER

INGREDIENTS:
1½ pounds chicken meat
   (boned and skinned), cut
   into strips ½ x ½ x 1½
   inches
1 Tablespoon cornstarch
5-6 scallions, cut in
   1½-inch pieces
Brown paper, cut in
   4-inch squares lightly
   oiled
Oil for deep-frying

MARINADE:
¼ teaspoon Five Spice Powder
4 thin slices ginger, minced
2 Tablespoons soy sauce
1 teaspoon brown sugar
salt and pepper

WOKCOOK:
1. Mix the chicken strips with the cornstarch, Five Spice Powder, minced ginger, soy sauce, sherry, sugar, and salt and pepper.

2. Place the paper on the surface in front of you so that it appears to be a diamond shape. Place one piece of coated chicken and 1 scallion piece across the paper, just below center. Fold the bottom third of the paper up and over the chicken. Over-lap both sides over the chicken. Secure the top of the envelope firmly into a slot cut into the paper.

3. Fry the parcels in hot oil for about 3 minutes. Drain and serve in the wrapper.

SESAME GREEN BEAN SALAD

INGREDIENTS:
1½ pounds young green
   beans, split and cut
   diagonally
1 Tablespoon oil

SEASONINGS:
1 teaspoon hot oil
2 cloves garlic, minced
½ teaspoon salt
1 Tablespoon soy sauce
½ teaspoon sugar
3 Tablespoons sesame seeds
   (toasted until golden)

WOKCOOK:

1. Heat the wok. Add the oil, hot oil, garlic, and beans. Lower heat and stir-fry for 2 minutes.

2. Add 1 Tablespoon soy sauce and 1 Tablespoon water. Cover and simmer for 3 minutes.

3. Place the beans in a dish and cool. Toss them with the sesame seeds and serve.

EGGPLANT IN GARLIC SAUCE

INGREDIENTS:
1 large eggplant, peeled and
   cut into ½-inch cubes
¼ pound beef, chopped
3 scallions, chopped
1 sweet red pepper, cubed
⅓ cup oil

SEASONINGS:
2 slices ginger, minced
3 cloves garlic, crushed

SAUCE:
1 teaspoon sugar
2 Tablespoons soy sauce
1 teaspoon salt
1 Tablespoon cornstarch
½ cup broth

WOKCOOK:

1. Heat the wok and add ⅓ cup oil, the eggplant cubes, and the sweet red pepper cubes.

2. When the eggplant and pepper appear softened, remove them from the wok.

3. Add the ground beef, ginger, and garlic. Stir-fry until the beef is lightly browned.

4. Mix the sugar, soy sauce, salt, cornstarch and broth. Add this to the beef and simmer until it thickens.

5. Return the eggplant and pepper to the wok. Heat thoroughly and serve.

ROAST PORK WITH BLACK BEAN SAUCE

INGREDIENTS:
½ pound roasted pork, cut
    into 1-inch pieces
½ pound snow peas
6 water chestnuts, sliced
1 small tomato, cut in
    ¼-inch slices
½ cup broth
2 teaspoons cornstarch
2 Tablespoons oil

SEASONINGS:
1 clove garlic, crushed
2 slices ginger, minced
1 Tablespoon sherry
1 Tablespoon sugar
1 Tablespoon soy sauce
1 Tablespoon black beans,
    washed and crushed
½ teaspoon sesame oil

WOKCOOK:

1. Heat the wok and add 2 Tablespoons oil, garlic, ginger, roast pork, snow peas, and waterchestnuts. Stir-fry for 1 minute on high heat.

2. Reduce the heat to medium and add the tomatoes. Cover and cook for two minutes.

3. Put the meat and vegetables on a warm platter.

4. Return the wok to a high heat. Mix the sherry, sugar, and black beans and stir-fry for 1 minute.

5. Mix the cornstarch and broth.

6. Add the cornstarch, broth, and soy sauce to the bean mixture and stir until slightly thickened.

7. Return the pork and vegetables to the wok and mix thoroughly.

Serve with steamed white rice.

9. COMPLETE DINNERS

The exotic sounding menus that follow are no more difficult to prepare than earlier menus. They are, however, a subtle sampling of some of the delicious, and healthy, Oriental recipes that will please all of your guests.

By now, I'm sure, many of the directions and procedures for preparation have become second nature to you. Your eye will become the best judge of the proper doneness of foods. Your experience will be able to evaluate what dishes go well together.

COMPLETE DINNER #1

Lotus Root Soup with Beef
Chinese Roast Pork
Bean Curd Casserole
Stir-Fried Zucchini and Tomato
Stuffed Shrimp with Bacon
Chicken with Walnuts
Sesame Peas and Water Chestnuts
Lion Head Pork Balls
Spicy Cold Noodles
Rice
Almond Cookies

LOTUS ROOT SOUP WITH BEEF

INGREDIENTS:
1 pound lotus root, peeled
   and thinly sliced
½ pound beef, shredded
2 whole scallions
6 cups beef broth

SEASONINGS:
1 slice ginger
1 Tablespoon soy sauce
salt and pepper

COOK:
1. Simmer the lotus root, beef, ginger, and scallions in the broth for 20 minutes.
2. Add the soy sauce. Cover and cook for 20 minutes more.
3. Remove the scallions and ginger slice discarding them.
4. Correct the seasoning and serve.

CHINESE ROAST PORK

INGREDIENTS:
2½ pound tenderloin of pork
or boneless loin of pork
cut into pieces 2 inches
square and as long as
possible

SEASONINGS:
⅓ cup hoisin sauce
2 Tablespoons soy sauce

MARINADE:
3 cloves garlic, crushed
½ cup soy sauce
⅓ cup sugar
1 teaspoon five spice powder
2 Tablespoons cognac or rum

COOK:
1. Coat the meat strips with marinade and let stand for 1 hour.
2. Preheat the oven to 400 degrees.
3. Remove the pork from the marinade and roast on a rack over a pan, turning and basting with a mixture of ⅓ cup hoisin sauce and 2 Tablespoons soy sauce.
4. Slice thinly and serve at room temperature.

BEAN CURD CASSEROLE

INGREDIENTS:
2 chicken legs and 1 whole
   chicken, chopped into
   1½-inch pieces
½ cup ham, shredded
½ cup shrimp, peeled and
   deveined
4 asparagus shoots, cut in
   1-inch pieces, (discard hard
   stems)
4 black mushrooms, soaked
   in boiling water for 15 to
   30 minutes and sliced
½ cup sliced bamboo shoots
3 fresh bean curd cakes, cut
   into 1-inch cubes

SEASONINGS:
1 Tablespoon sherry
1 teaspoon salt
¼ teaspoon pepper
2 Tablespoons soy sauce

COOK:

1. Place the chicken pieces and salt and pepper in a large dutch oven and cover with water. Bring to a boil and simmer for 1 hour.

2. Add the ham, shrimp, asparagus, mushrooms, and bamboo shoots and simmer for ½ hour more.

3. Add the bean curd, sherry, and soy sauce. Cook five minutes longer and serve in a casserole.

STIR-FRIED ZUCCHINI AND TOMATO

INGREDIENTS:
4 cups zucchini, cut in
   ¼-inch slices
2 tomatoes, peeled, seeded,
   and cubed
6 water chestnuts, sliced
2 cups finely shredded
   spinach
2 Tablespoons oil

SEASONINGS:
1 clove garlic, crushed

SAUCE:
½ cup broth
2 teaspoons sherry
½ teaspoon sugar
2 teaspoons cornstarch
salt and pepper

WOKCOOK:
1. Mix the sauce.
2. Heat the wok and add the oil and garlic. Cook for 15 seconds.
3. Add the zucchini and stir-fry for 2 minutes, then add the tomatoes and chestnuts.
4. Stir-fry for 1 minute and add the sauce. When it is piping hot and thickened, pour it over the finely shredded spinach and serve.

STUFFED SHRIMP WITH BACON

INGREDIENTS:
16 Jumbo shrimp
16 slices bacon
12 water chestnuts, minced
1 cup breadcrumbs
4 scallions, minced

SEASONINGS:
1 slice ginger; minced
3 cloves garlic, minced
1 teaspoon Chinese parsley
2 Tablespoons lemon juice
1 Tablespoon soy sauce
   salt and pepper

113

COOK:

1. Preheat the oven to 400 degrees F.
2. Put the shrimp in a saucepan and cover with water. Bring to a boil. Immediately, rinse the shrimp with cold water, and peel and devein.
3. Mix the water chestnuts, breadcrumbs, scallions, ginger, garlic, parsley, and lemon juice, making a paste.
4. Cut the shrimp lengthwise but not completely through, so that each shrimp will be split but still in one piece. Fill the cavity with 1½ Tablespoons of the paste.
5. Wrap a slice of bacon around the shrimp.
6. Place the shrimp on a rack over a 2-inch-deep pan.
7. Brush them with soy sauce and cook them until the bacon is almost crisp, turning once and brushing with the soy again.
8. Put on a warm platter and garnish with Chinese parsley.

CHICKEN WITH WALNUTS

INGREDIENTS:
2 whole chicken breasts,
  boneless and skinless,
  cubed in 1-inch pieces
½ cup bamboo shoots
1 scallion, chopped in 1-inch
  pieces
¼ cup chicken broth
1½ cup walnut halves
oil for deep-frying

SEASONINGS:
2 slices of ginger, minced
1 teaspoon sesame oil

MARINADE:
1 teaspoon sugar
2 teaspoons soy sauce
2 Tablespoons sherry

WOKCOOK:

1. Blanch the walnuts and deep-fry them until golden.
2. Add the sugar, soy sauce, and sherry to the chicken.
3. Heat the wok and add 2 Tablespoons oil. When it starts to smoke, add the ginger, stir-frying a few seconds.
4. Add the chicken and stir until it loses its pink color.
5. Add the bamboo shoots and scallions. Cook 1 minute more.
6. Add the broth. Cover and cook on medium heat for 2 minutes.
7. Stir in walnuts and sesame oil. Serve immediately.

SESAME PEAS AND WATER CHESTNUTS

To brighten any tasty platter

INGREDIENTS:
Garden peas, steamed
Sliced water chestnuts

SEASONINGS:
1 teaspoon sesame oil
salt & pepper

COOK:

1. Add the sesame oil to the steamed vegetables. Season to taste.
2. Serve on warmed platter or beside a spicy dish.

LION HEAD PORK BALLS

INGREDIENTS:
1½ pound lean pork, minced
6 black mushrooms, soaked
   15 to 30 minutes in boiling
   water and minced
10 water chestnuts, minced
5 scallions, minced
1 egg, lightly beaten
2 teaspoons cornstarch
Oil for deep frying
1½ cups chicken broth
¾ pound spinach, washed,
   drained, stems removed,
   and cut into 3-inch pieces

SEASONINGS:
2 garlic cloves, crushed
3 thin slices ginger, minced
3 Tablespoons sherry
salt and pepper

SAUCE:
2 Tablespoons soy sauce
1 Tablespoon vinegar
2 teaspoons cornstarch
4 Tablespoons water

COOK:

1. Mix the minced pork, mushrooms, chestnuts, scallions, garlic, and ginger with the sherry, 2 teaspoons cornstarch, and egg.

2. Divide mixture into 8 portions and form balls for deep frying.

3. Heat the oil and deep-fry the pork balls for 4 minutes until lightly browned. Remove them from the oil and drain.

4. Heat the broth in a large pan and put in the meatballs. Cover and simmer for 20 minutes.

5. Place spinach on top of the meatballs and simmer for 10 minutes.

6. Remove the spinach and arrange it on a platter. Place the pork on top of the spinach.

7. Mix the sauce ingredients and add to the broth. Thicken and pour over the meatballs and spinach.

SPICY COLD NOODLES

INGREDIENTS:
½ pound fresh lo mein
4 cups bean sprouts
½ cup shredded, cooked ham

SEASONINGS:
1½ teaspoon sesame oil
4 Tablespoons wine vinegar
4 Tablespoons soy sauce
2 teaspoons hot oil

COOK:
1. Bring 4 quarts of water to a boil and drop in the noodles. Cook for 7 to 10 minutes or until tender.
2. Drain and rinse with cold water.
3. Toss with the sesame oil and refrigerate.
4. Cook the bean sprouts in boiling water for 30 seconds. Rinse with cold water and drain.
5. Combine all ingredients, toss, and serve cold.

ALMOND COOKIES

INGREDIENTS:
1 cup lard
1 cup sugar
1 teaspoon almond extract
1 egg
2½ cups flour
1½ teaspoon baking soda
½ teaspoon salt
¾ cup blanched, slivered almonds
¼ cup sliced almonds
1 egg, lightly beaten

117

COOK:

1. Beat the lard and sugar until it is fluffly.
2. Add the almond extract and egg and continue beating.
3. Sift together the baking soda, salt, and flour, and add it gradually to the dough.
4. Mix in the almonds.
5. Roll walnut-sized balls and press them flat on a cookie sheet.
6. Brush them with the lightly-beaten egg and place a sliced almond on top.
7. Bake at 350 degrees for 20 minutes.

Makes 3-4 dozen cookies.

COMPLETE DINNER #2

Celestial Soup
Cold Peppered Pork
Poached Chicken and Walnut Salad
Stir-Fried Szechwan Celery
Asparagus with Crab Sauce
Beef with Oyster Sauce
Deep Fried Sea Bass with Sweet and Sour Sauce
Pork with Fried Noodles
Rice
Watermelon and Lychee

CELESTIAL SOUP

INGREDIENTS:
¼ cup spinach, chopped
3 scallions, chopped
6 cups water

SEASONINGS:
2 Tablespoons soy sauce
¼ teaspoon sesame oil
1 teaspoon salt

COOK:
1. Bring the water to a boil. While this is being done, mix all the remaining ingredients.
2. Pour the boiling water over the greens. Wait a few minutes and serve.

COLD PEPPERED PORK

INGREDIENTS:
1½ pound pork loin whole, boneless
2 scallions

SEASONINGS:
3 thin slices ginger, minced
2 teaspoons salt
¼ teaspoon crushed red pepper flakes

SAUCE:
2 Tablespoons soy sauce
2 teaspoons vinegar
3 teaspoons sesame oil
1 Tablespoon hot oil
4 cloves garlic, very finely minced
1 teaspoon sugar
6 small pieces parsley

COOK:

1. Cover the pork with water in a large saucepan or wok. Add the seasonings (not the sauce) and cover and boil until tender. Depending on the thickness of the meat, this will take about 45 minutes to 1 hour.

2. Remove the pork from the broth and cool for at least one hour.

3. During this time, mix the sauce.

4. Cut the pork in very thin slices and then into shreds, double matchstick size. Arrange side by side in a rectangular pile.

5. Pour the pepper sauce over it.

POACHED CHICKEN AND WALNUT SALAD

INGREDIENTS:
1 whole chicken breast, skinned and boned
½ cup broth
1½ cups Chinese cabbage, shredded
1 cup watercress (stems removed)
1½ cups lettuce, shredded
1 cup walnuts, blanched and deep-fried until golden

SEASONINGS:
1 garlic clove, minced
1 Tablespoon vinegar
juice of 1 large orange
1 Tablespoon soy sauce
¼ teaspoon "hot oil"

DRESSING:
3 Tablespoons rice white wine
1 Tablespoon soy sauce
1 Tablespoon sugar
½ teaspoon salt
few drops of sesame oil

COOK:

1. Simmer the chicken with the broth, garlic, vinegar, orange juice, soy sauce and hot oil until tender (20-30 minutes).

2. Cool and cube the chicken.

3. Toss the other ingredients and the dressings.

STIR-FRIED SZECHWAN CELERY

INGREDIENTS:
4 cups celery, cut diagonally
  in ¼ inch slices
¼ cup sweet red peppers
2 scallions, chopped
2 Tablespoons oil

SEASONINGS:
6 Szechwan peppercorns
1 Tablespoon sherry
1 teaspoon sugar
2 Tablespoons soy sauce

WOKCOOK:
1. Heat the wok and add the oil. When it begins to smoke, add the peppercorns. Stir them briefly to flavor the oil, then discard them.
2. Add the celery, sweet pepper, and scallions to the wok. Stir-fry them for 1 minute.
3. Add the remaining seasonings and cook for 1 minute longer and serve.

ASPARAGUS WITH CRAB SAUCE

INGREDIENTS:
½ cup crab meat, cooked and
  shredded
½ cup light cream
2 eggs, lightly beaten
1 Tablespoon oil
1 pound cleaned and steamed
  asparagus

SEASONINGS:
1 Tablespoon lemon juice
1 teaspoon dry mustard
½ teaspoon sugar
⅛ teaspoon "hot oil"

COOK:
1. Heat all the ingredients and seasonings except the asparagus in the top of a double boiler stirring constantly.
2. When the sauce has thickened, pour it over the asparagus and serve.

BEEF WITH OYSTER SAUCE

INGREDIENTS:
1½ pound trimmed steak, cut
  in ¼ inch slices
5 scallions split lengthwise
  and cut in 1 inch pieces
1 cup fresh mushrooms,
  sliced
½ cup bamboo shoots
½ cup chicken broth
1 Tablespoon cornstarch
3 Tablespoons oil

SEASONINGS:
3 slices ginger
1 clove garlic, minced
¼ cup oyster sauce

MARINADE:
1 Tablespoon dark soy sauce
2 Tablespoons sherry
1 teaspoon sugar
½ teaspoon "hot oil"
1 Tablespoon vegetable oil

WOKCOOK:
1. Marinate the cut steak for 30 minutes.
2. Drain the steak, reserving the marinade.
3. Heat the wok and add 2 Tablespoons oil. Cook the garlic and ginger for 30 seconds.
4. Sauté the beef, stirring for 2 minutes or until it is cooked according to doneness preferred. Remove the beef from the wok and drain in a seive-lined bowl.
5. Fry the scallions, mushrooms, and bamboo shoots for 30 seconds in the remaining 1 Tablespoon oil.
6. Dissolve the cornstarch in the chicken broth and add to the wok. Also add the oyster sauce and marinade. Cook it until thickened, then add the beef.
7. Heat thoroughly and serve.

Garnish with shredded carrots and chopped parsley.

DEEP FRIED SEA BASS WITH SWEET AND SOUR SAUCE

INGREDIENTS:
2½ pound sea bass, cleaned
   and dried (scored 8 times
   on each side)
½ cup cornstarch
½ cup green sweet peppers,
   diced
½ cup bamboo shoots, slivered
6 water chestnuts, sliced
3 scallions, split lengthwise
   and cut into 1 inch pieces
½ cup tomato chunks (tomato
   peeled and seeded)
Oil for deep-frying

MARINADE:
1 Tablespoon sherry
1 Tablespoon soy sauce
2 thin slices ginger, minced

SAUCE:
1 cup wine vinegar
1 cup brown sugar
2 Tablespoons cornstarch

WOKCOOK:
1. Rub the fish with the marinade and let stand for 30 minutes.

2. Dry the fish and coat it lightly with cornstarch.

3. Heat the wok and add the oil. Place the fish on a seive and lower into the oil. Deep-fry a few minutes, until done. Drain the fish and place it in a warm oven.

4. In a clean wok, heat 2 Tablespoons oil and stir-fry the green peppers, bamboo shoots, water chestnuts, scallions, and tomato chunks for 1 minute.

5. Heat the sauce to a boil and cook until thickened.

6. Re-fry the fish in the first wok, then cover with the sauce and vegetables and serve.

PORK WITH FRIED NOODLES

INGREDIENTS:
½ pound noodles (cake form),
   soaked in boiling water to
   loosen and drain
6 black mushrooms, softened
   with boiling water and sliced
¼ pound pork, thin sliced
½ cup bean sprouts, root tip
   removed
2 cups spinach, chopped in 1
   inch pieces
2 scallions, chopped
Oil for deep frying

SEASONINGS:
4 teaspoons soy sauce

SAUCE:
1 cup broth
1 Tablespoon cornstarch

WOKCOOK:

1. Deep-fry the noodles until golden. Remove from the oil.

2. Drain all but 1 Tablespoon oil from the wok. Stir-fry the pork and the soy sauce for 3 minutes.

3. Add the bean sprouts, spinach, and a mixture of broth and cornstarch. Bring it to a boil to thicken.

4. Add the scallions and bean sprouts and pour over the noodles.

WATERMELON AND LYCHEES

INGREDIENTS:
1 watermelon
1 can lychees with syrup
1 can pitted cherries
1 can Mandrarin oranges
1 cup pineapple chunks
canned loquats, drained (optional)
canned kamquats, drained (optional)

124

MIX:

1. Split the watermelon and remove the seeds. Remove the pulp and make 1-inch melon balls.

2. Mix the melon balls with the other fruits and put them in the watermelon shell.

3. Spoon the lychee syrup over the fruit and serve.

COMPLETE DINNER #3

Winter Melon Soup
Barbequed Spareribs
Poached Chicken with Ginger and Scallions
Broccoli with Vegetables
Crispy Fish with Three Vegetables
Red Cooked Duck with Cabbage
Szechwan Beef with Scallions
Shrimp Noodles with Vegetables
Rice
Toffee Apple and Banana Fritters

WINTER MELON SOUP

INGREDIENTS:

1 winter melon the size of a a volleyball: cut off top (1½ inches), remove the seeds, and clean the inside of the melon

3 pints of chicken broth, boiling hot

¼ cup bamboo shoots, shredded

¼ cup diced water chestnuts

4 black mushrooms, pre-soaked and sliced

¼ cup ham slivers

1 chicken breast, diced

½ cup shrimp, peeled, de-veined, and cut in half

1 Tablespoon cornstarch in ¼ cup water

salt and pepper

125

1 Tablespoon sherry
salt and pepper

COOK:

1. Use a soup kettle or pot large enough to steam the melon. Place a rack on the bottom and the melon on top of it.
2. Fill the melon ¾ full with the broth. Replace the melon top.
3. Pour 1 inch of boiling water around the melon and steam 3½ to 4 hours over medium heat. Add more water to the pot if necessary.
4. Mix all the remaining ingredients and add to the melon.
5. Replace the lid and continue to steam 1 to 2 hours until the melon pulp is soft and translucent but not mushy.
6. To serve, secure the melon in a dish to hold it. Serve from the melon.

Serves 8 to 12

BARBEQUED SPARERIBS

INGREDIENTS:
3 pounds lean spareribs

MARINADE:
3 Tablespoons soy sauce
⅛ teaspoon Five Spice Powder
⅓ cup hoisin sauce
4 thin slices ginger, minced
2 Tablespoons vinegar
3 Tablespoons honey
1 Tablespoon sherry
1 clove garlic, crushed

COOK:

1. Combine the marinade and pour over the spareribs in a long flat dish or pan. Marinate for several hours.

2. Cook over charcoal or in an oven preheated to 325 degrees. Hang the spareribs with "S" hooks in the oven over a foil lined pan with ½ water in it.

3. Roast slowly for 1 hour.

4. Raise the heat to 450 degrees and roast 15 minutes longer or until the ribs are crisp and golden brown.

5. Serve hot or at room temperature, with plum sauce.

POACHED CHICKEN
WITH GINGER AND SCALLIONS

INGREDIENTS:
1 whole chicken
⅓ cup oil

SEASONINGS:
1 teaspoon sesame oil
4 Tablespoons thinly sliced and peeled ginger, minced
4 scallions, cut in 1 inch lengths and cut once lengthwise
4 Tablespoons soy sauce
1 Tablespoon sugar
1 Tablespoon sherry

COOK:

1. Poach the chicken covered with the water for 30 minutes or until tender.

2. Drain, cool, and dry the chicken.

3. Rub the chicken with sesame oil and cut into serving pieces.

4. Heat the wok and add the oil. Cook the scallions and ginger for 30 seconds.

5. Add the soy sauce, sugar, and wine to the oil. Heat for 1 minute and pour over the chicken.

6. Serve a little cooler than room temperature. Garnish with pineapple and watercress.

BROCCOLI WITH VEGETABLES

INGREDIENTS:
4 cups broccoli florets
1 cup water chestnuts, cubed
   (⅜ inch)
1 cup shredded carrots,
   (matchstick size)
2 cups Chinese cabbage, shredded
3 Tablespoons oil

SEASONINGS:
1 Tablespoon soy sauce
1 Tablespoon sherry
½ teaspoon sugar
salt and pepper to taste

WOKCOOK:
1. Heat the wok and add the oil. When the oil begins to smoke, add the broccoli, and stir-fry for 2 minutes.
2. Add the waterchestnuts and carrots. Lower the heat, cover, and cook for 5 minutes.
3. Add the cabbage and seasonings, stir-fry for 1 minute, and serve.

CRISPY FISH WITH THREE VEGETABLES

INGREDIENTS:
2 to 3 pound fish (sea bass
   or red snapper), cleaned
1 egg, lightly beaten
¼ cup cornstarch
1 cup carrots, shredded
1 cup celery, shredded
2 chopped scallions
Oil for deep frying

SEASONINGS:
2 Tablespoons black beans,
   washed and crushed
1 teaspoon sliced ginger,
   minced
3 cloves garlic, crushed
1 Tablespoon sherry
1 cup broth
2 Tablespoons soy sauce
2 Tablespoons oyster sauce
½ teaspoon sugar
½ teaspoon hot oil
1 Tablespoon cornstarch
2 Tablespoons water

WOKCOOK:

1. Coat the fish with egg. A few minutes later, lightly coat it with cornstarch.

2. Deep fry the fish until golden. Drain and place the fish on a warmed platter.

3. Remove all but 1 Tablespoon oil from the wok. Stir-fry the carrots and celery for 30 seconds. Turn down the heat and cover and cook for 2 minutes. Then remove the vegetables from the wok and arrange them over the fish.

4. Add 1 teaspoon oil to the wok. Stir-fry the black beans, sherry, ginger, and garlic for 1 minute. Add the scallions and remaining seasonings. Bring to a boil and pour the sauce over the fish.

Serve immediately

RED COOKED DUCK WITH CABBAGE

INGREDIENTS:
1 duck, 4 to 5 pounds, dried
   with excess fat removed
4 cups Chinese cabbage,
2 black mushrooms, softened
   in boiling water and sliced
Oil for deep-frying
2 teaspoons cornstarch plus
   enough to coat duck for
   deep frying

MARINADE:
1 Tablespoon soy sauce
1 Tablespoon sherry
½ teaspoon salt

SAUCE:
3 Tablespoons soy sauce
3 cups water
¼ teaspoon five spice powder
1 teaspoon orange peel

COOK:

1. Rub the inside and outside of the duck with the marinade.

2. After several hours lightly coat duck with cornstarch and deep-fry it until golden.

3. Place the sauce ingredients in a large pan with the duck. Simmer for 2 hours or until tender. The bones should pull out of the meat easily.

4. Place the duck on a flat surface. Cut it in half lengthwise through the back. Remove all the bones, keeping the skin intact.

5. Press the duck into a small, shallow bowl and steam for 15 minutes.

6. Heat the wok. Add 1 Tablespoon oil and stir-fry the cabbage and mushrooms for 2 minutes.

7. Invert the duck onto a platter and put the cabbage around it. Use 2 teaspoons cornstarch dissolved in 2 Tablespoons water to thicken some of the sauce in which the duck was simmered.

8. Pour the sauce over the duck and garnish with parsley.

SZECHWAN BEEF WITH SCALLIONS

INGREDIENTS:
¾ pound flank steak, sliced
   thinly across the grain
6 scallions, cut in 1½ inch
   pieces and split
4 black mushrooms, soaked in
   boiling water and sliced
½ cup oil

SEASONINGS:
4 garlic cloves, minced
1 slice ginger, minced
2 Tablespoons soy sauce
1 teaspoon sesame oil

MARINADE:
2 Tablespoons sherry
2 Tablespoons soy sauce
1 teaspoon sugar
½ teaspoon ground szechwan
   pepper
1 Tablespoon oil

WOKCOOK:

1. Marinate the beef for 15 to 30 minutes.
2. Heat the wok and add the oil. When it begins to smoke, add the garlic and ginger.
3. Pour off the marinade and with the mushrooms, stir-fry the beef, cooking the beef to the doneness that you prefer.
4. Quickly add the scallions, 2 Tablespoons soy, and 1 teaspoon sesame oil.

Serve with rice.

SHRIMP NOODLES

INGREDIENTS:
½ pound shrimp, peeled,
   deveined and chopped
1 scallion, chopped
1 egg white

SEASONINGS:
½ teaspoon ginger root,
   minced
2 Tablespoons sherry
1 teaspoon sugar
2 Tablespoons milk

COOK:

1. Put the above ingredients except for the shrimp in the blender and puree.

2. Strain the liquid and return to the blender with the shrimp. Blend into a paste.

3. Bring 2 quarts of water to a boil. Put the puree mixture into a pastry bag with a small tip and squeeze into the boiling water.

4. When the noodles float to the top, remove and drain them.

SHRIMP NOODLES WITH VEGETABLES

Use the above recipe for shrimp noodles and combine them with these colorful ingredients.

INGREDIENTS:
½ cup carrots, shredded to
    matchstick size
1 cup peas
½ cup shredded ham
1 cup bean sprouts
2 eggs, lightly beaten
¼ cup chicken broth
3 Tablespoons oil

SEASONINGS:
1 clove garlic, crushed

WOKCOOK:

1. Heat the wok and add 1 Tablespoon oil. Add the garlic, carrot shreds, and peas. Cook for 2 minutes and remove from the wok.

2. Put the remaining 2 Tablespoons oil in the wok and stir-fry the eggs gently. Add the vegetables, ham, bean sprouts, and noodles, and broth. Heat thoroughly and serve.

TOFFEE APPLE AND BANANA FRITTERS

INGREDIENTS:
2 apples, cored and peeled,
   cut into 10 pieces
1 banana, sliced in ½ inch
   pieces
½ teaspoon grated orange peel
1 cup self-rising flour
1⅓ cup water
1 Tablespoon oil
oil for deep-frying
bowl of ice water

SYRUP:
½ cup sugar
2 Tablespoons water
1¼ Tablespoons water
1½ Tablespoons sesame seeds

COOK:

1. Mix grated orange peel, self-rising flour, and cornstarch and make a well in the center. Pour 1⅓ cup water into the well. Add 1 Tablespoon oil and mix.

2. Coat the fruit with the batter and deep-fry until golden.

3. Make the syrup by heating the sugar and water until the sugar has dissolved. Add the oil, continuing to heat until the sugar carmelizes and turns light brown.

4. Stir the fried fruit into the syrup and add sesame seeds.

5. Serve on lightly oiled plates.

6. The fruits should be dipped in the ice water for the carmel to harden.

10. GOURMET DINNERS

I'd like to call this chapter, "One Step Beyond." It will truly take you one step beyond the typical recipes that you have tried. Some of the ingredients may be more difficult to locate. If you have a Chinese specialty shop in your area, you may be able to find what you need.

The *Hot Pot* recipe is especially enjoyable to prepare and eat. It's the oriental version of fondue — but much more subtle.

GOURMET DINNER #1

Birds Nest Soup
Rolled Chicken with Lettuce
Peking Duck
Shrimp Mixed Salad
Sweet and Sour Pork
Sauteed Sliced Fish with Baby Corn
Chinese Cabbage Hot Salad
Rice
Peking Dust
Keemum Tea

BIRD'S NEST SOUP

INGREDIENTS:
¼ pound bird's nest, soaked
  overnight, feathers and
  debris removed
¼ pound cooked chicken, shredded
¼ pound cooked ham, shredded
2 egg whites, lightly beaten
6 cups chicken broth

SEASONINGS:
salt to taste

135

COOK:

1. Bring the broth to a boil and add the soaked bird's nest. Simmer for 30 minutes.

2. Add the chicken and ham shreds and return the mixture to a boil.

3. Stir in the egg whites and salt in a slow stream. Cook until the egg whites are set.

ROLLED CHICKEN WITH LETTUCE

INGREDIENTS:
2 whole chicken breasts, thinly
   sliced and shredded
2 red chili peppers, shredded
2 green chili peppers, shredded
8 water chestnuts, sliced
8 to 10 lettuce leaves, washed
2 Tablespoons oil

SEASONINGS:
1 garlic clove, crushed
2 slices ginger, minced

MARINADE:
2 teaspoons cornstarch
1 egg white
1 Tablespoon sherry
½ teaspoon sugar

SAUCE:
½ cup broth
2 teaspoons cornstarch
1 Tablespoon soy sauce

WOKCOOK:

1. Mix the chicken in the marinade and let stand for 30 minutes.

2. Heat the wok and add the oil, garlic, and ginger. Cook for a few seconds.

3. Add the chicken shreds. Stir-fry until it is white and add the chilies and water chestnuts.

4. Stir-fry for 1 minute more and remove from the heat.

5. Put a small portion of this mixture in each lettuce leaf and roll up the leaf.

6. Place the lettuce rolls in a shallow dish.

7. Reheat the wok and heat the sauce until it thickens. Pour it over the lettuce rolls and serve.

PEKING DUCK

INGREDIENTS:
1 duck, 5 to 6 pounds, (preferably a Long Island duck), washed and dried
1 bunch scallion flowers
1 recipe chinese pancakes
1 cucumber peeled and cut into strips ¼ inch x ½ inch x 2 inches

SEASONINGS:
1 Tablespoon rice wine or sherry
1 teaspoon salt
2 Tablespoons honey
½ cup hoisin sauce
1 Tablespoon sesame oil

COOK:
1. Bring a large deep pan of water to a boil. Dip the duck in boiling water 1 minute, remove and pat dry. Rub the inside with 1 Tablespoon wine and 1 teaspoon salt.

2. Place uncovered on a rack at the bottom of the refrigerator, or hang in a cool place, for one day to dry.

3. On the second day, glaze with a mixture of 2 Tablespoons honey and ⅓ cup water. Refrigerate 1 more day and cook on a rack over a pan according to the following schedule.

400 degrees for 10 to 20 minutes
350 degrees for 25 minutes
300 degrees for 20 minutes
250 degrees until it appears done
450 degrees to brown

4. Preparation for serving:
Cut one bunch of scallions into 2 inch pieces. Slit the ends and place in ice water to curl.
Make Chinese Pancakes and steam them just before serving.
Mix prepared Hoisin Sauce with 1 Tablespoon sesame oil.

5. To serve:
Carve the duck into thin slices and cut the skin into strips. Drain the scallions and serve separately with the sauce and cucumber strips.
In the middle of the pancake, place a piece of the duck, a scallion flower dipped in the sauce, and a cucumber strip. Roll the pancake and serve.

SHRIMP MIXED SALAD

INGREDIENTS:
1 pound small shrimp, peeled, and deveined
4 black mushrooms, soaked in boiling water for 15 to 30 minutes and sliced
1 medium zucchini, cut across in ¼ inch slices
1 cup shredded bok choy hearts
½ cup bamboo shoots, cut to double matchstick size
¼ cup carrots, shredded
½ cup bean sprouts
¼ cup chicken broth
2 Tablespoons oil

SEASONINGS:
1 clove garlic, crushed

SALAD DRESSING:
2 Tablespoons oil
2 Tablespoons vinegar
1 teaspoon sesame seeds, crushed
1 Tablespoon soy sauce
½ teaspoon dry mustard
¼ teaspoon M.S.G.
¼ teaspoon black pepper
¼ teaspoon salt

WOKCOOK:
1. Mix the salad dressing.

2. Heat the wok and add 2 Tablespoons oil and the garlic. Cook the garlic 15 seconds and add the shrimp.

3. Stir-fry the shrimp until they turn pink and remove them from the wok.

4. Put the mushrooms, zucchini, bamboo shoots, and carrots in the wok and toss quickly for 1 minute on medium high heat. Add the broth, bok choy hearts, and bean sprouts. Cook for 15 to 30 seconds until they begin to soften.

5. Toss together the shrimp, vegetables, and salad dressing. Serve at room temperature.

SWEET AND SOUR PORK

INGREDIENTS:
Cube 1 pound lean pork
¾ cup cornstarch
3 cups oil for deep frying
4 dried mushrooms soaked in
  boiling water for 15 to 30
  minutes.
1 small green pepper, cubed
1 small red pepper, cubed
1 yellow onion cut in ¾-inch
  cubes
½ cup pineapple, fresh or
  canned chunks
1 tomato cut in 1 inch cubes
⅓ cup bamboo shoots, sliced
  thinly

SEASONINGS:
2 cloves garlic, chopped
3 slices ginger, chopped

MARINADE:
1 Tablespoon soy sauce
¼ cup sugar
1 Tablespoon rice wine
  or sherry

SAUCE:
1½ cups water
¾ cup sugar
3 Tablespoons cornstarch,
  dissolved in ½ cup water
½ cup cider or red wine
  vinegar
2 Tablespoons soy sauce

WOKCOOK:

1. Marinate pork with 1 Tablespoon soy sauce ¼ cup sugar, 1 Tablespoon rice wine or sherry.

2. Spread wax paper or plastic wrap on flat surface and spread ¾ cup cornstarch over it. Roll pork in cornstarch until it is moist and no white cornstarch can be seen. Deep-fry in the wok until golden brown and completely cooked. Drain and place on a platter in warm oven.

3. Mix the sauce ingredients. Heat to a boil and cook until thickened.

4. Pour off all but 2 Tablespoons oil from the wok and add garlic and ginger. Swirl around and add the vegetables.

5. Stir-fry until the onions start to become clear at the edges (3 to 5 minutes).

6. Meanwhile, re-heat sauce. Add to cooked vegetables and stir the mixture for 30 seconds.

7. Pour the sauce over the pork and serve immediately.

139

SAUTEED SLICED FISH WITH BABY CORN

INGREDIENTS:
¾ pound fish fillets, sole or flounder, cut in 1½ inch squares
¼ cup bamboo shoots, thinly sliced
1 small can baby corn
¾ cup snow peas, slivered and shredded
1 Tablespoon cloud ear, soaked and sliced
¼ cup oil

SEASONINGS:
3 slices ginger, minced
1 clove garlic
½ cup stock
¼ teaspoon salt

MARINADE:
1 Tablespoon cornstarch
2 teaspoons sherry
½ teaspoon sugar

WOKCOOK:
1. Place the fish in the marinade.
2. Heat the wok and add 2 Tablespoons oil. When it begins to smoke, add the garlic.
3. Stir a few times and add the vegetables, cloud ear, sugar, and liquids. Cover and cook for 2 minutes.
4. Remove the vegetables and sauce from the wok and add the remaining oil and the salt and ginger.
5. Cook this for 15 seconds and stir-fry the fish pieces until done, 3-5 minutes. Return the vegetables and sauce to the wok. Heat thoroughly and serve.

CHINESE CABBAGE HOT SALAD

INGREDIENTS:
1 medium head Chinese cabbage, cut in ½ inch slices
4 black mushrooms, presoaked and sliced, stems removed
6 water chestnuts, coarsely chopped
½ cup bamboo shoots, shredded
2 scallions, chopped
2 Tablespoons oil

SEASONINGS:
1 clove garlic, crushed
4 slices ginger, minced
½ teaspoon salt
½ teaspoon sesame oil

WOKCOOK:

1. Heat the wok and add the oil, garlic, and ginger. Stir-fry for a few seconds.

2. Add the mushrooms, waterchestnuts, bamboo shoots, and scallions. Stir for 1 minute.

3. Add the cabbage and salt. Stir until it is tender but crisp. Sprinkle with the sesame oil and serve immediately.

PEKING DUST

INGREDIENTS:

1 cup shelled pecans
½ cup sugar
oil for deep frying

1 can chestnuts (marrons)
1 Tablespoon brown sugar
1 pint heavy cream
¼ cup confectioners sugar

COOK:

1. Pour boiling water over the pecans and let stand for 5 minutes.

2. Drain the pecans and coat them with ½ cup sugar. Spread them to dry for approximately 30 minutes.

3. Deep-fry the pecans and spread on a greased plate to cool.

4. Purée the chestnuts in a blender. Add the brown sugar and mix well.

5. Whip the cream and gradually fold in the confectioners sugar.

6. Mix one half of the whip cream with the chestnut purée and place this in the serving dish. Put the remaining whipped cream on top and sprinkle with the sugared pecans.

GOURMET DINNER #2

Shark Fin Soup
Chinese Dumplings
Three Green Vegetables
Szechwan Bean Curd
Butterfly Shrimp with Vegetables
Chicken Velvet
Lotus Root Salad
Chestnuts with Beef
Lobster Fried Rice
Rice
Coconut Float
Dragon Well Tea

SHARK FIN SOUP

INGREDIENTS:
½ pound package of shark fin
   needles, soaked overnight
½ pound chicken breasts,
   boned, skinned and
   shredded
½ cup ham, minced
½ cup bamboo shoots, cut
   in thin strips ½-inch wide
1 scallion, chopped
4 cups broth
2 Tablespoons oil

SEASONINGS:
2 slices ginger
1 Tablespoon sherry

MIX:
1 Tablespoon soy
1 Tablespoon sherry
1 Tablespoon cornstarch
1 Tablespoon water

WOKCOOK:

1. Drain the soaked shark fins and put them in boiling water with the sherry and 1 slice of ginger. Simmer for two hours.

2. Drain the fins and rinse them with cold water. Save the "needles". (These are the gelatinous protuberances from the fin.)

3. Heat the wok and add the oil. When it begins to smoke, add the 2nd ginger slice. Stir for a few seconds, then discard the ginger.

4. Add the chicken shreds and stir-fry for 1 minute.

5. Stir in the chicken broth and shark fin needles. Simmer for 30 minutes.

6. Add the ham and bamboo shoots. Cook for 5 minutes longer.

7. Stir in the cornstarch mixture and scallions. Continue stirring until the soup has thickened. Serve.

CHINESE DUMPLINGS

INGREDIENTS:
1 package dumpling skins
  (90-100)
1½ pound ground pork
4-6 black mushrooms, soaked
  for 30 minutes in boiling
  water and minced
½ cup bamboo shoots, minced
½ pound bean sprouts, minced
2 leaves Chinese cabbage,
  minced
1 cup Chinese chives (can be
  replaced with scallions and
  more garlic)
1 egg
1 beaten egg

SEASONINGS:
3 cloves garlic
1½ teaspoon soy sauce
1 Tablespoon fresh ginger,
  minced

143

WOKCOOK:

1. Chop up all the vegetables finely and squeeze them hard to remove the excess water.

2. Combine all the seasonings and ingredients except the skins, and mix well.

3. Place about 1 heaping teaspoon of the mixture in the center of the dumpling skin.

4. Brush the edge of the skin with beaten egg and fold in half, pressing the edges together. With 2 Tablespoons of sesame oil in the skillet, brown the dumpling on both sides. Add ½ cup water and quickly cover the skillet and simmer about 10 minutes or until all the water evaporates.

Serve with soy sauce, sesame oil, hot oil, and vinegar, mixed. As an alternative deep-fry the dumplings and serve with mustard mixed with soy sauce as a hot hors d'oeuvres.

THREE GREEN VEGETABLES

INGREDIENTS:
2 cups green beans, shredded
   as in "French cut"
1 sweet green pepper,
   shredded
3 cups celery, strings
   removed and thinly sliced
1 Tablespoon peanut oil

SEASONINGS:
1 slice ginger, minced
salt

SAUCE:
2 Tablespoons sherry
1 teaspoon sugar
¼ cup broth
2 teaspoons cornstarch

WOKCOOK:

1. Heat the wok and add 1 Tablespoon oil. When it begins to smoke, add the ginger, stirring a few seconds.

2. Stir-fry the green beans and sweet peppers for a few seconds until they turn bright green.

3. Stir in the celery and cook 30 seconds.

4. Mix the sauce and add to the wok. Stir until thickened and serve.

SZECHWAN BEAN CURD

INGREDIENTS:
½ pound ground pork
6 squares bean curd, cut in
   1-inch squares and well-
   drained
½ cup scallions, chopped
1 Teaspoon vegetable oil

SEASONINGS:
1 large clove garlic, minced
2 slices ginger, minced
1 Tablespoon sherry
2 teaspoons hot pepper oil
1 teaspoon crushed red
   pepper flakes
2 Tablespoons soy sauce
1 teaspoon sesame oil

SAUCE:
¼ cup chicken broth
½ teaspoon sugar
1 Tablespoon cornstarch

WOKCOOK:

1. Heat wok and add the oil. When it begins to smoke, add the garlic and ginger. Cook 30 seconds.

2. Add the ground pork and stir-fry until light brown and dry.

3. Add the sherry, hot pepper oil, crushed red pepper, and soy sauce.

4. Add the bean curd and scallions, stirring gently 1 minute.

5. Mix and add the sauce. Thicken and serve the bean curd with sesame oil sprinkled on top.

BUTTERFLY SHRIMP WITH VEGETABLES

INGREDIENTS:

12 jumbo shrimp, peeled and
 deveined cut lengthwise
 almost in half to make a
 cavity for the meat
12 slices ham, cut the length
 of the shrimp
12 slices bacon, cooked and
 cut to the size of the shrimp
2 eggs, lightly beaten
3 Tablespoons flour
1 Tablespoon cornstarch
Oil for deepfrying and stir-
 frying
2 large onions, cut in large
 chunks
1 sweet red pepper, cut in
 chunks and parboiled

SEASONINGS:

1 clove garlic

SAUCE:

¼ cup ketchup
1½ Tablespoons worcester-
 shire sauce
2 teaspoons sugar
½ cup water
1 Tablespoon soy sauce
1 teaspoon cornstarch
1 Tablespoon vinegar

COOK:

1. Make a batter with the 2 eggs, 3 Tablespoons flour and 1 Tablespoon cornstarch.

2. Fit the ham and bacon in the middle of the slit shrimp.

3. Heat oil for deep-frying and dip the shrimp carefully in the batter and deep-fry 2 to 3 minutes. Drain the shrimp and place on a warm platter.

4. Remove all but 1 Tablespoon oil from the wok. Heat the wok until the oil smokes. Stir fry the garlic, onion, and sweet red pepper until the onion starts to appear translucent around the edges.

5. Place these vegetables on the bottom of a serving dish.

6. Mix the sauce ingredients and heat until slightly thickened.

7. Add the shrimp, heat until piping hot, and pour over the vegetables.

CHICKEN VELVET

An elegant dish which is a specialty of the Shantung Province in Northern China.

INGREDIENTS:
1 whole chicken breast.
  remove tendons, cube, and
  put into blender with:
 cup chicken broth
1 Tablespoon cornstarch
1 cup and 1 Tablespoon oil
½ cup bamboo shoots,
  shredded to matchstick size
½ cup ham, minced
½ frozen peas
2 scallions, cut in ¼" pieces

SEASONINGS:
1 Tablespoon sherry

WOKCOOK:
1. Purée the chicken broth and cornstarch in a blender.
2. Heat oil in wok and pour in chicken slowly. Cook until opaque. Stir very slowly. Pour off excess oil and remove to a heated dish.
3. Heat 1 Tablespoon oil in wok and add bamboo shoots, peas, and ham. Stir-fry for 1½ minutes.
4. Return chicken to the wok and add 1 Tablespoon sherry and scallions.

LOTUS ROOT SALAD

INGREDIENTS:
1 pound lotus root, peeled,
  cut in quarters lengthwise,
  and thin sliced
¼ cup carrot, shredded

SEASONINGS:
1 teaspoon salt
1 Tablespoon sugar
2 Tablespoons vinegar
2 Tablespoons soy sauce
½ teaspoon "hot oil"
½ teaspoon sesame oil
1 Tablespoon peanut oil

COOK:
1. Sprinkle salt over the sliced lotus root, cover with water, and let stand for 20 minutes.
2. Drain the lotus root and rinse the salt off with boiling water. Put the carrots and lotus root in boiling water for several minutes, then drain.
3. Mix the seasonings and toss with the lotus root and carrots.
4. Chill and serve.

CHESTNUTS WITH BEEF

The smoked flavor of the chestnuts will compliment the beef.

INGREDIENTS:
4 cups shredded flank steak
½ pound dried, skinned chestnuts, simmered for 1 hour
  in a covered pan with 3 cups
  water, cut them in half
1 cup broth
1 Tablespoon oil
2 teaspoons cornstarch
1 pound green beans (French
  style cut), steamed

SEASONINGS:
¼ cup soy sauce
3 Tablespoons sherry
1 Tablespoon brown sugar
1 teaspoon sesame oil
1 teaspoon sesame seeds

148

WOKCOOK:

1. Heat the wok. Add 1 Tablespoon oil and sauté the beef until it loses the pink color.

2. Add the chestnuts, soy sauce, sherry, brown sugar, and ¾ cup broth. Cover and simmer for 20 minutes.

3. Mix ¼ cup broth with the cornstarch and add to the simmering mixture the last few minutes.

4. Steam the green beans and toss with the sesame oil.

5. To serve, place the beef in the center of the platter and the beans around it. Sprinkle the beans with sesame seeds and sesame oil.

LOBSTER FRIED RICE

INGREDIENTS:
1½ cups cooked and cooled
    rice (see recipe)
6 ounces cooked and flaked
    lobster
3 chopped shallots
2 tomatoes, peeled, seeded,
    and chopped
2 eggs, slightly beaten
2 Tablespoons oil
¼ cup shredded ham
1 scallion, split lengthwise
    and cut in 1-inch pieces

SEASONINGS:
1 Tablespoon soy sauce

WOKCOOK:

1. Heat the oil in a wok. Add the chopped shallots and cook 30 seconds. Add the eggs and cook until they are half set.

2. Add the rice and stir-fry until the grains are coated with the egg.

3. Stir in the cooked lobster, tomatoes, and soy sauce.

4. Serve in a warmed dish garnished with the ham and scallions.

COCONUT FLOAT

INGREDIENTS:
1 Fresh coconut, meat removed
    from the shell and the brown
    peel removed
1 cup water
1 cup milk
4 Tablespoons sugar
1 package unflavored gelatin
Mandarin oranges, canned
pitted cherries, canned
lychees, canned
bananas, sliced

COOK:

1. Put the coconut and water in a blender or food processor to purée.

2. Steep the coconut in the water and milk for 10 minutes.

3. Extract the liquid from the coconut pulp by wrapping it in cheesecloth and squeezing. Discard the pulp.

4. Soften the gelatin in ¼ cup water.

5. In the meantime, mix the fruits and chill.

6. Heat the gelatin, sugar, and coconut milk until the gelatin dissolves.

7. Pour the liquid into a square 8 inch cakepan to set. Cut the set coconut gelatin into squares to float on top of the fruit mixture.

GOURMET DINNER #3

Stuffed Walnut Crab Claws
Spring Rolls
Hot Pot
Fried Walnuts
Sweet Orange Tea
Jasmine Tea

STUFFED WALNUT CRAB CLAWS

Add water chestnut flour to the batter for extra crispness.

INGREDIENTS:
12 crab claws
1½ pound shrimp, shelled,
   deveined and minced
½ cup chopped walnuts
¼ cup cornstarch

SEASONINGS
3 teaspoons salt
¼ teaspoon pepper

BATTER:
1 teaspoon cornstarch
1 scallion, minced
1 egg
1 teaspoon soy sauce
1 teaspoon sherry

WOKCOOK:

1. Boil 3 cups of water in a wok with 2 teaspoons salt and cook the crab claws. When done, remove to a platter to cool. Remove the shell to expose the crab meat, leaving the shell intact on the top 1-inch of the claw.

2. Combine the minced shrimp with 1 teaspoon salt, ¼ teaspoon pepper, and 1 Tablespoon cornstarch.

3. Mix the batter, combining 1 teaspoon cornstarch, scallion, soy sauce, sherry, and egg.

4. Lightly coat the crab meat with cornstarch. Press 1 Tablespoon of the shrimp mixture into each side of the claw. Dip the claw into the batter, roll in walnuts and deep fry for 2 to 3 minutes.

Serve with duck sauce and mustard.

151

SPRING ROLLS

INGREDIENTS:

1 cup pork, roasted and
   finely diced
1 cup shrimp, peeled, cooked,
   and finely diced
6 black mushrooms, pre-
   soaked, and finely chopped
½ cup celery, minced
1 cup bok choy, shredded
4 scallions, chopped
1 cup bean sprouts
1 egg, lightly beaten
8 to 10 egg roll or spring
   roll wrappers
Oil for deep frying

SEASONINGS:

1 Tablespoon soy sauce
1 teaspoon salt
½ teaspoon sugar

WOKCOOK:

1. Heat 2 Tablespoons oil in the wok. Add the pork, shrimp, mushrooms, celery, bok choy, and scallions. Stir-fry for 2-3 minutes.

2. Add the bean sprouts and seasonings. Remove from the heat.

3. Place the egg roll or spring roll on a flat surface. Put about ¼ cup of filling in the center.

4. Form the egg roll as follows:

   a. Fold the bottom corner up with the tip a little above the center.

   b. Fold both side corners in over the tips overlapping about ½ to ¾ of an inch.

   c. Roll down the top corner and seal with the egg.

5. Heat oil for deep-frying. Cook 2 to 3 eggrolls at a time until golden-brown and crisp.

6. Drain and serve at once with duck sauce and mustard.

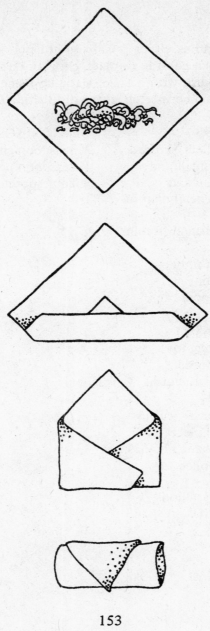

HOT POT

This recipe requires either a Chinese hot pot, electric wok, or fondue pot. Each guest has a plate, chopsticks, soup bowl, soup spoon, a small dish with a sauce made up of equal parts of soy sauce, sherry, and cornstarch, also a dish with a raw egg.

INGREDIENTS:
½ pound fish fillets, skinned
　　and cut into small pieces
12 shrimp, peeled and
　　deveined and nearly cut in
　　half.
2 chicken breasts, cut in thin
　　slices
1 pound steak, thinly cut
　　across the grain
½ pound mushroom caps,
　　thinly sliced
1 cup cubed eggplant
2 cups cherry tomatoes
1 package snow peas
2 bean cured cakes, cut in
　　1-inch cubes
1 cup spinach leaves, cut in
　　medium-sized pieces
4 ounces cellophane noodles,
　　soaked and boiled for
　　2 minutes
¼ cup chopped scallions
6 to 8 cups broth

SEASONINGS:
¼ teaspoon ginger, minced
½ teaspoon pepper
1 Tablespoon sherry

COOK:

1. Bring the broth, ginger, pepper, and sherry to a boil in the pot.

2. Each guest puts one or two of the raw pieces in the broth and cooks it to his or her taste, usually about 1 minute.

3. The meat and vegetables may be dipped in a cornstarch mixture before cooking. After cooking, the guest can dip the food in the raw egg and then use one of several sauces provided as seasoning.

4. After the meats and vegetables have been cooked, the boiled noodles, spinach, bean curd, and chopped scallions should be put into the broth.

This mixture is then served in the bowls.

SAUCES:

Hoisin sauce
Mustard/soy sauce
Soy sauce/vinegar/hot oil

Duck sauce
Ginger/soy sauce

FRIED WALNUTS

INGREDIENTS:
2 cups walnuts
2 Tablespoons lemon juice
2 Tablespoons honey
¾ cup sugar
Oil for deep frying

COOK:

1. Blanch walnuts with boiling water and remove skins.

2. Cover walnuts with lemon juice, honey and boiling water\ and let stand for 2 minutes.

3. Drain the walnuts and mix with the sugar to coat. Let stand several hours until dry.

4. Deep fry until golden brown.

SWEET ORANGE TEA

INGREDIENTS:
4 oranges, the pulp and fruit only (remove membranes)
¼ cup orange juice
3 Tablespoons cornstarch
⅔ cup sugar
5 cups water
¼ cup pineapple chunks
¼ cup red grapes, cut in half and seeds removed

COOK:
1. Mix the sugar, cornstarch, and water. Bring it to a boil and thicken.
2. Add the fruit and heat. Do not cook the fruit.

Serve in cups or bowls.

11. INGREDIENTS

It would be an enormous task to list every Chinese ingredient. Those presented in this list represent ingredients used in the recipes in this book. A few additional ingredients commonly considered part of the Chinese chef's larder are also included.

INGREDIENT TIMETABLE

Perishable

Immediate use, up to one week

Bamboo shoots, fresh
Bean Curd Cake
Bean Sprouts
Bitter Melon
Bok Choy
Celery Cabbage
Chili Peppers
Chinese Parsley
Chinese Cabbage
Chinese Chives
Fuzzy Melon
Ginger, fresh
Lichee
Long Beans
Lotus Root
Mustard Greens
Scallions
Snow Peas
Water Chestnuts, fresh
Winter Melon

Moderately Perishable

Good for about 10 days when canned items are opened. Place food in glass jars in refrigerator

Bean Sauce
Chili Paste
Chinese Roast Pork, frozen
Chinese Sausage, frozen
Egg Roll Wrappers, frozen
Hoisin Sauce
Pickled Scallions
Plum Sauce
Sesame Paste
Vegetables, frozen
Won Ton Wrappers, frozen

Stored For Several Months

Includes unopened canned items

Abalone, canned
Baby Corn, canned
Bamboo Shoots, canned
Bean Sauce, canned
Bird's Nest, dried
Black Beans, dried
Black Mushrooms, dried
Cellophane Noodles, dried
Chestnuts, dried or canned
Chili Paste, canned
Chinese Parsley, dried
Cloud Ear, dried
Five Spice powder
Hoisin Sauce, canned
Hot Dried Red Pepper

Hot Oil
Lily Buds, dried
Lotus Root, canned
Mustard Powder
Sesame Oil
Sesame Paste, canned
Sesame Seeds
Shark's Fins
Soy Sauce
Star Anise
Straw Mushrooms, canned
Szechwan Peppercorns
Tangerine Peel
Tree Ear Mushrooms
Water Chestnuts, canned

INGREDIENTS

Ingredients	Other Names	Description
Abalone		*The firm, thin, flesh of a deep-sea shellfish that may be purchased in cans. Once opened it can be stored in the refrigerator 4 days, in a tightly covered jar, in its own liquid.*
Baby Corn	*Young Corn* *Sweet Young Corn*	*Miniature ears of corn 2½ inches in length sold in jars.*
Bamboo Shoots	*Juk Soon*	*These are ivory-colored vegetables, usually purchased canned. This is one of the most used and basic Chinese vegetable. If you are lucky enough to find the vegetable fresh in a Chinese market it will look almost like a sweet potato. It must be peeled and the hard tips removed. The recipes in this book assume that you are using canned bamboo shoots, which are partially cooked. Fresh ones require a longer cooking period.*

Bean Cake
Bean Curd
Tofu
Dow Fu

A white, fragile, custard-like pad made from soy beans. You may not like it the first time you try it. It is available in cans, but fresh bean cake is preferable. If fresh, it will keep only a few days in the refrigerator and it must be covered with clean water each day.

Bean Sauce, Brown

Made with yellow beans, this salty, spicy, thick paste is used for meats and vegetables alike.

Bean Sauce, Yellow
Whole Bean Sauce
Mein See

A thick yellow bean by-product of soy sauce. It may be purchased in jars or cans and will keep for months when it is stored in a covered jar in the refrigerator. A substitute would be Japanese miso.

Bean Sprouts
Mung Bean Sprouts
Dou Neja

A white, crisp, thread-like vegetable about 1½ to 2 inches long, produced from many beans. Bean sprouts become brownish when bruised and stale. Only the freshest white sprouts should be used in cooking and the cooking time should never exceed 1 minute.

Bird's Nest
Swallow's Nest
(dried)

These small light gelatinus bird's nests have the appearance of shredded coconut and they must be soaked and cleaned. They are a rare delicacy.

Bitter Melon   Foo gwa

A green vegetable which resembles a cucumber in size and shape. It has a pebbly, shiny skin which is left on for serving. The seeds and pulp, however, should be removed before cooking. It is usually blanched to remove the bitter taste and cooked with bean sauce for flavoring.

Black Beans   Dow See, Fermented Salted Black Beans

Tiny, soft, salty black beans which are exclusive to Chinese cooking. They are washed, mashed, and usually combined with garlic and ginger for use in meat and seafood recipes. You may substitute brown bean sauce.

Black Mushrooms

Available in all sizes. Usually they are blackish with a wrinkly outside and a light underside. They must be soaked in boiling water for 15 to 30 minutes and the stems discarded before use.

Bok Choy

A long, dark, leafy green vegetable with white stalks. The appearance is somewhat like Swiss chard.

Celery Cabbage

The long, green cabbage usually found in super- markets. Most dishes require the use of the stalks (hearts) only since the tender leaves wilt quickly when cooked. The leaves can be used in salads nd soups.

163

Cellophane Noodles	Bean Thread Long Rice Transparant Noodles Vermicelli	*White, dry, thin noodles made from ground mung beans. They must be soaked before cooking, at which time they become transparant. They tend to stick together when cooked and are difficult to eat with any finesse unless they are broken into small pieces prior to soaking.*
Chili Paste	Szechwan Paste	*This is a very hot paste composed of crushed garlic and hot peppers. An acceptable substitute is 1 Tablespoon bean sauce, ¼ teaspoon powdered red pepper, 1 large clove of garlic, crushed, and a pinch of salt.*
Chili Peppers	Hot Peppers Chilies	*Dark green or red, from 2 to 6 inches in length approximately ½ inch in diameter, and used only in very spicy dishes. A substitute would be dried hot peppers.*
Chinese Parsley	Cilenetra Coriander Leaves Yuen Sai	*The stems and size are similar to American type parsley, although the leaves are larger and serrated. The taste however is different. It is aromatic, strong, and pungent.*

164

Chinese Cabbage

This vegetable is similar to celery cabbage and bok choy. It is a thicker, shorter head than the celery cabbage and lighter in color. If Chinese cabbage is unavailable, celery cabbage or young American cabbage may be substituted.

Chinese Chives

These chives have a stronger taste than American chives. They are available in Chinese markets during the late spring and early summer. At other times of the year, you may substitute scallions and a little garlic in recipes that require this ingredient.

Chinese Dates   Jujube nuts

Small, dried, wrinkled fruits the size of a red grape. They must be soaked overnight and they are used to add sweetness to a recipe or mixed fruit.

Chinese Roast Pork

Many recipes call for roast pork. If you do not want to spend the time and effort to first roast the pork and then prepare the dish, you may wish to purchase the already roasted pork from the Chinese market or the delicatessen. It is sold in completely cooked strips or slices.

Chinese Sausage	Lop Cheung	Sold in pairs, these slender, 6-inch sausages are made from pork. They are cut in thin slices and steamed or cooked on top of rice.
Cloud Ear Mushrooms	Black Fungus Wan Yee	Small, brown-black dried fungus, which must be soaked and triple in size. They have a mild pleasant flavor.
Dried Chestnuts		Conveniently peeled, these chestnuts must be soaked overnight or broiled 1½ hours (for 1 cup) before they are used in a recipe. Fresh chestnuts may be substitutes if they are boiled and peeled.
Dried Shrimp		These small, dried shrimp have a salty and intense flavor. They should be soaked and used in small quantities.
Egg Roll Wrappers	Spring Roll Skins	These are very thin, square pastry sheets made with flour, eggs, and water. Seal them and store them frozen until they are ready to use. If they are not wrapped securely they will dry out and break when you handle them.

Hot Oil

This is oil cooked with hot, dried red peppers. It is red in color and adds a hot spicy flavor instantly to any recipe. It can be made with the following recipe: Heat ⅓ cup vegetable oil in a small pan. When it starts to smoke, stir in 2 Tablespoons crushed hot red pepper flakes or 3 Tablespoons powdered hot red pepper.

Lichee
Lichee nuts

Red pebbled skin and a white translucent sweet pulp, this succulent fruit is eaten chilled.

Lily Buds
Tiger Lily Stems
Gum Jum

These golden brown, 2-inch flower buds must be soaked prior to use and the hard ends should be discarded.

Long Beans

Long green beans, that have the appearance of a foot-long string bean. They are usually cut into small, 2-inch sections for cooking. Chinese markets have them in late summer and early fall.

Loquats

This is a small yellow apricot-like fruit.

Lotus root

Reddish brown on the outside and creamy white inside. There are holes tunneling through the crisp six to eight inch roots which form an interesting pattern when the roots are sliced.

Mung beans

Very tiny green pea-like bean. Can be sprouted for bean sprouts.

Mustard

Hot Chinese mustard is prepared by mixing 1 Tablespoon of dried mustard powder with a little boiling water to make a thin paste. Then add ¼ teaspoon oil, ¼ teaspoon vinegar, and a pinch of salt. Let it stand for 30 minutes until it loses the bitter taste.

Mustard Greens

This bright green, leafy vegetable with thick curved stems has a bitter taste. It is most commonly used for soups and as a pickled vegetable.

Oyster Sauce

Thick, dark brown sauce made from oysters and soy sauce. Frequently used as a seasoning or condiment, it has no fishy odor as the name would imply

Pickled Scallions

These small, white, pickled bulbs of scallions are a delightful addition to a sweet and sour recipe. With the tangy pickled flavor, they may be also used as a decorative relish.

Plum Sauce

A brownish chutney-type sauce made from plums, apricots, vinegar, and sugar. It is used as both a seasoning and condiment.

Preserved Vegetable

A heavily salted, preserved vegetable which is used in soups and stir-fried dishes.

Rice Powder

Rice Flour

Flour made from raw rice. It imparts an interesting flavor when it is substituted for part of the flour in Chinese pancakes and other pastries.

Scallions

Green Onions
Spring Onions

Long, tender, mild onions that are white at the bottom and green at the top. They are used whole or in pieces (roots removed) in Chinese recipes and as a garnish.

Sea Cucumber

Sea Slug

This black mollusk is between 4 and 5 inches in length. It is sold packaged and considered a great delicacy.

Sesame Oil

Strong, brownish oil with a nut-like flavor, usually a seasoning rather than a cooking oil. When a recipe requires sesame oil you cannot omit it without significantly altering the subtle flavor of the dish.

Sesame Paste

A dark, beige-colored paste made from white sesame seeds. Middle Eastern Tahini paste is a reasonable substitute. It can be stored for several months in a refrigerated glass jar.

169

Sesame Seeds   Very small, black or white seeds. The black and white seeds can be mixed to give the dish an interesting appearance.

Shao Hsing Wine   White rice wine frequently used in Chinese. A dry sherry is a good substitute.

Shark's Fin   A cleaned, dried, boneless shark's fin should be pale in color. This is a delicacy which is used for festive occasions.

Snow Peas   This bright green, flat pod is delicate and tender. The tip is broken and the string pulled away.

Soy Sauce   There are numerous brands of soy sauce available. Some are imitation flavor, and some are authentic and made from soybeans. The latter is much preferred. Types of soy sauce range from light and thin to dark and heavy-flavored black types with carmel color added. Lighter soy sauce is desirable with vegetables and when a more subtle flavor is required. Dark soy sauce is used in some meat and some soup recipes to provide a strong rich flavor. However, you should try a variety of brands and decide which ones suit your taste.

Star Anise

This dried seed, shaped like an eight pointed star, is used for a licorice-flavored spice in meat and chicken recipes.

Straw Mushrooms

Having the appearance of a droopy fragile mushroom, these brown and white delicate mushrooms are frequently used in seafood and vegetable dishes.

Sweet Cucumbers *Sea Melons*

These are small, thin, little cucumbers, 2 to 3 inches long. They have a sweet flavor and a crunchy texture. They are used both as an ingredient and as a condiment.

Szechwan Peppercorns

Reddish crushed peppercorns. They add a distinct spicy flavor to Szechwan dishes.

Tangerine Peel

This is a dried bittersweet peel which must be soaked before it is used in poultry dishes.

Tree Ear Mushrooms

These mushrooms are black, dried, and more delicate than cloud ear mushrooms. They are usually measured by the spoon while still dried and then soaked for use in a recipe.

Water Chestnut Powder   *A flour made from water chestnuts. Used with cornstarch to give a crunchy coating on deep-fried foods.*

Water Chestnuts   *Grown in water, these chestnuts resemble the brown chestnuts before they are peeled for use. They are white and crunchy in texture on the inside. When fresh, they discolor unless they are immediately covered with water. Canned, peeled, whole water chestnuts are readily available in almost every supermarket.*

Winter Melon   *A large, squash-type vegetable with a slight green rind and a white meat. The size varies from the size of a large honey dew melon to pumpkin size. It can be purchased whole, by the pound, or by the slice. The seeds should be removed before it is used in a recipe.*

Won Ton Wrappers   *Very flat, round or square noodles, which can be filled and used for soup or an appetizer. They may also be fried and sprinkled with sugar for dessert.*

178

179

180

Additional Notes and Recipes

Additional Notes and Recipes

Additional Notes and Recipes

Additional Notes and Recipes

Additional Notes and Recipes

Additional Notes and Recipes

Additional Notes and Recipes

Additional Notes and Recipes

Additional Notes and Recipes

Additional Notes and Recipes